Bird of Paradox

and Other Tales

John Devlin

Paperback

ISBN: 978-1-918039-04-7

Cover design by: Cathy Bonner

Published by: Good Reach Publishing

Acknowledgements

First, my thanks to Cathy Bonner for her brilliant work on the cover and her creative input throughout. I'm also grateful to Stephen Brown and the team at the publishers for their guidance and belief in this project from the start.

To my friends and family, thank you for your ongoing support, patience, and encouragement, especially during the moments when the stories refused to behave.

Finally, I dedicate this book to my dear friend Tony Desmond. Tony had a life-changing accident some time back and is still in recovery. Yet he remains a force behind these pages.

Table of Contents

Author's Note

It has taken me a long time to consider publishing these stories.

I've always written things down—whether as notes or diary entries—because things happen when you take the roads less travelled. And I've learned that chance is a fine thing: so many forks in the road, so many conservative choices that could have led to lifelong cul-de-sacs.

This erratic path took me to many strange corners, from a semi-settled life in rural Ireland all the way to China & Vietnam, teaching English.

Meanwhile I (mis)spent my time looking for ladies in all the wrong places, and socialising with a plethora of interesting eccentric people I would otherwise never have had the opportunity to meet.

Each tale here began as a scrap of overheard gossip, a scribbled note, or the kind of boast a man makes when all bets are off. Some are funny, some are decidedly not, and most linger in the murky space where the ridiculous and the tragic rub shoulders. I've changed a few names and compressed a few timelines, but the bones of these stories are real. If you took the Long An bus in 2020, you might recognize the conductor. If you've ever lingered in Tooting Broadway, you'll definitely know the smell.

So why share them now? To preserve the memories—the things that happened on the way to the fair, the faces that surfaced in my travels, the mornings I still wake up half-convinced I'm in Starbucks in Taojin,

Guangzhou or Highlands Coffee in Saigon. Writing is the only way to hold onto the feeling without booking another ticket.

You can dip into these stories at random, but I've arranged them as a loose journey: London to China, south into Vietnam, with detours to Ireland in between. Let the ticket stubs lie where they fall.

Thanks for picking up the book. If any of these wanderings sparks a laugh, a wince, or the sudden urge to pack a bag- then just follow your curiosity…..

John Devlin

Part One

Home Front

Bird of Paradox

For Barry, the weekend was usually a time to relax and mooch around, but not today. Here he was on a Saturday morning, up at the crack of dawn, off on a mission – but not one of his own choosing.

It was his mother, she who must be obeyed. She had been at him for weeks, most recently two days before.

"Barry, you haven't visited your Aunt Lena since God knows when!"

"I know, Mother, but I've been busy."

"I've asked you several times."

"It's not as if Huntingdon is just up the road."

"You're hardly that busy. You're her only close relative over there. She keeps asking why you haven't been to see her."

"Wasn't she over in Ireland for a few weeks?"

"Well, she's back in Cambridgeshire now."

No point arguing; he knew she wouldn't take no for an answer.

He sighed. "Okay. Tell her I'll be there on Saturday."

Too late he remembered his girlfriend's birthday party that same evening. It was going to be one busy day.

And so the conflicted voyager set off. He first took the Tube from Tooting Broadway to King's Cross. Even though he had been in London for some time, the Underground was still a shock to the system. There was no getting used to Tube culture; the studied indifference of the early-morning travellers was always something to behold. It was back in the days before the smartphone. Many passengers were reading the free *Metro* newspaper; others had brought their own. The carriage had a kind of library atmosphere.

One never got into conversation on the Tube – not that he was in the mood. No eye contact, no talking, eccentrics and oddballs aplenty. At the weekend there was always a chance of spotting the men with the curly shoes, but not today. However, to make up for their absence, a few seats away sat an African man dressed all in black and wearing a stovepipe hat.

His thoughts switched to Lena – such a snob. How had he allowed his mother to talk him into this? Even thinking about Lena was stressful. He always felt uncomfortable around her; she put him on edge. She annoyed him at times. So insincere. Sometimes very sweet, other times a total bitch. She had a habit of mirroring people she had just met, then cutting them to pieces behind their backs.

At King's Cross he switched from the Tube to main-line rail. When he entered the compartment there were already two people inside, a male student and a man of about sixty. The student was busy reading a textbook and the older man had the do-not-disturb look about him. Two large suitcases sat on the rack above. The older man had a healthy tan, suggesting a recent arrival from sunnier climes.

Just before they set off, two middle-aged ladies entered and sat together.

"What a pleasant surprise to bump into you, Fiona," said the taller of the two. She spoke so softly Barry could hardly hear her.

"It's well over a year since I last saw you, Mabel," said the other lady, who spoke with a Scottish accent.

"Doesn't time fly," replied Mabel.

"I seem to recall your son was just home from Australia."

"Ah, yes. I hadn't seen him in six years."

"You remember old Mrs Brooks – suffering from some form of cancer."

"Poor dear. Is it progressive?"

"I just know she's having chemotherapy at the moment. I hope she pulls through."

"I go to the gym, try to keep fit – best way to stay healthy," said Mabel.

"Yes, me too. My problem is that the course I want to do runs at lunchtime, which doesn't suit me."

Barry had been half listening, half day-dreaming. As the ladies drew breath, reality returned. How was Lena going to be today? Different days brought different moods. He just knew he had to be prepared for anything. 'Eccentric' was one word that came to mind. How could he minimise the length of stay? He would try not to be rude, but he needed to get back early – it was Ellie's birthday and he still had to buy the flowers.

"What's your husband up to, Mabel, now he's retired?" enquired Fiona as the ladies resumed their conversation.

"Dan was always a DIY enthusiast. Now he's busy doing up the kitchen. He recently finished widening the drive."

"My Noel is a keen gardener. Where I can, I help too. He does the digging and weeding; I focus more on the design."

"Do you still go to the same church, Fiona?"

"Yes, the RC one on Monastery Road."

"Our Irish neighbour, James Quinn, goes there."

"Gosh, I know James well. He plays cards with my husband."

"Isn't it a small world."

"After we retired, we bought a house near our church."

"That sounds ideal. As you know, ours is a bit away – at least it's not a problem while we're still mobile."

Soon after, Mabel got off at Welwyn. They promised to keep in touch. The younger man also left the train.

Lena was liable to rant about any number of diverse topics. He was sure to hear about her ex, her youngest daughter who was on a multitude of drugs, her brother's fancy woman and the offspring of that relationship. If she was in a bad humour her attention could turn to Arabs, Jews, Indians, paedophiles, family, or the neighbours back in Ireland (who were all stupid).

Other hardy annuals included sickness, death, diseases, hospitals, churches, cemeteries and such like.

It wasn't so bad if she happened to be in a middling humour; she was liable to orate on comets, evolution, earthquakes, nuclear bombs, Neanderthal man, literature or American politics. On a really good day there would be talk of her friend Farmer Coyle, her animals and her farm. The thought caused him to shudder.

At Stevenage, Fiona got off. Two new ladies came on board, one fairly hefty, the other thin and sickly-looking. They sat silently for a few minutes. Once the train was in motion they were soon nattering away, totally oblivious to everything around them. They discussed upcoming holidays and the difficulties of selling flats in Marbella.

"Martha, I'm worried about my cat," said the sickly-looking one.

"What's wrong, Janet?"

"He has a thyroid problem. I can't bear to think of losing him. He was such a beautiful cat."

Janet described the cat's colour, age, size and temperament.

"Now he has lost weight and his hair is falling out."

Janet must have seen Barry grimacing. She shot him a very sharp look. She didn't realise it had little to do with her or her cat. Barry had been reminded of his aunt and her herd of feline friends. One was called Mr Pussy, named after an Irish drag artist often referred to as 'Ireland's leading misleading lady'. One day Lena fed some leftover beans to Mr Pussy. A short time later the cat started to fart. Every time he took a step he farted; every time he farted he stopped and looked behind him. Rinse and repeat.

By the time the train reached Sandy, Barry was the only passenger left in the carriage. Not far to go now. Watching and listening to his fellow travellers had been some distraction. Time had passed quickly. He felt a little more relaxed and not quite so pessimistic.

As well as being eccentric, Barry was well aware that Lena was unpredictable, enigmatic and without either morals, manners or scruples. Hadn't she once had an affair with a priest? And hadn't the neighbours nicknamed the son McTaggart?* If she had a problem with anyone, her first instinct was to consult a lawyer. She never took responsibility for anything and all accidents and mishaps were laid at the feet of others.

Barry couldn't stop thinking about Lena's chequered history, from her humble beginnings to marrying an oil magnate. Perhaps her persona had changed to match her lifestyle when she married old Gerrit. She had moved from working as a nurse to being the wife of an amputee with a plethora of servants, housekeepers, vehicles and chauffeurs at her beck and call.

The lady had entered a world that was all about affluence, money and power. She loved to reminisce about her married days when she was welcomed in high society. When Gerrit divorced her, everything changed; those doors were all closed to her. But she still loved to talk about those she described as 'wealthy'. Indeed, she still referred to the old boy as her husband. She was in her element name-dropping and speaking knowingly about property tycoons, the gentry, the intelligentsia and people with PhDs.

When Lena paused, Barry never knew whether to agree, disagree or say nothing. He usually just suffered in silence. On one occasion, when he failed to react, she advised him to see a therapist. Any intervention at all could set her off in another direction with renewed enthusiasm, vigour, and often venom, directed at whichever individual or group came to mind.

Tales of improbable friends were a constant. One of these was a lady she met regularly for coffee – her last remaining link to her lost world. For these dates Lena would spend hours preening and primping in advance. She saw herself as a bird of paradise. Her daughter once referred to her as 'more like an old bird of paradox'.

This friend in Leighton Buzzard had reputedly seen off three husbands and amassed a large property empire in the process. She was then undone by a toyboy. Not only had the young man emptied her bank accounts, he had also tried to orchestrate a situation where she would fall off a hotel balcony. Miraculously, she survived, albeit with a broken ankle.

Finally, the train pulled into Huntingdon. It was wild and wet outside, raining 'pussies and poodles', as Lena might say. Time to face the music. Sure enough, she was standing on the platform, her long grey hair flying in the breeze. Barry was greeted with a long embrace followed by smiles all round.

She looked him up and down. "You're looking well, Barry – and you've lost weight."

"I go to the gym twice a week."

"I feel so small beside you."

Despite the weather, she seemed in good humour. Barry was relieved but knew things could change in an instant.

When they arrived back at her house Barry was introduced to her new dog, a red setter.

"This is Rusty. I've only had him for two weeks."

"What happened to Muldoon?"

"He had to be put down. Sure you saw him yourself – he was on his last legs. He was eighteen."

"What about Mr Pussy? I heard he was off beans for Lent?"

"Yes, most definitely. One feed did him."

"How many cats have you now?"

"Four that I know of. Actually, I'm a bit puzzled – they've been eating a lot more food recently."

"Worms?"

"I don't think so. I suspect there are one or two dinner guests who arrive regularly and unannounced."

"Maybe you need to stand guard at mealtimes?"

"I don't have the patience."

Lena made coffee. Lunch would come later. And so it began. The first topic was her nursing career. Barry knew what to expect: these tales were always of the bizarre variety and laced with lots of sexual allusions.

First up was the story of a man who arrived in casualty when she was nursing in Navan. This man, known as The Major, was in great pain. Apparently, he had put boiling water into his sex doll. As a result, his private parts were badly scalded. Her colleague had to hold his member while Lena applied cream. Lena claimed The Major roared like a bull while the treatment was being applied.

Then there was the story of the brothel in Athboy which was frequented by the boys in blue. On one occasion the Chief of Police was on duty there. Whatever happened, he and the dispenser of emergency love got stuck and couldn't be separated. Both had to be brought into casualty and disunited there – no doubt slightly embarrassing. Barry had heard this story several times now, although the one about the Major was new to him.

There was a fly buzzing around the room. Lena had a thing about insects. Barry was reminded to keep all doors and windows closed. There had always been an obsession with flies, spiders and moths. She would make regular tours of the house, fly-swatter in hand, exterminating all bugs in her path.

Even in mid-conversation, if she saw a fly inside, she wouldn't rest until she had hunted it down. This morning she sat watching a fly on the outside of the window for rather a long time. Out there it didn't bother her.

"I've never seen one like this before – look at its two white paws."

Barry chuckled but said nothing. It reminded him of a story his mother told about when she was young and they were all at home. One night they were watching an action film on TV. The hero was about to be shot.

Lena shouted, "It's OK, here comes a helicopter."

There was a daddy-long-legs on the screen.

From her talk it appeared that Lena had come into a large sum of money recently. The source wasn't disclosed. There was speculation on how she might spend it. She had a farm near Dublin and spent most summers there. At times she favoured buying tractors; at others there were beef houses being built, greenhouses erected, vegetables and herbs grown – all organic, of course.

Lena was cooking while these topics were aired. After a time, braised steak and vegetables were served, followed by apple crumble and custard. Barry ate and she talked. She only ate a little herself, picking at her food like a sparrow.

Inevitably, old Gerrit came up in the conversation, as if he were still in her life. Today was no different. She had heard he was having a lot of mishaps recently. He had nearly fallen out of his wheelchair while being hoisted onto an aeroplane; he had been left dangling by the safety straps for several minutes until they brought him back to earth.

"I heard you were back in Ireland recently," ventured Barry.

"Yes, had some business to attend to." She didn't go into details.

"Did you see all the family?"

"Some of them. Nothing much changes."

"They're all doing well, then?"

"Yes, I suppose so. I spent a day with my brother Olly over in Summerhill. A strange household."

"How do you mean?"

"They live their lives without ever reading a book. The wife goes to bingo regularly, never cooks. The two boys are obsessed with rally cars. Aaaagh! Uncultured!"

"Everyone has their own tastes," he suggested, trying not to aggravate the situation.

"And I suspect not one of them darkens the door of either church or chapel!"

Barry thought it better to leave it at that.

When she saw Barry had nothing more to say about the family, Lena moved on to her horses. Two were in training down near Delvin in Westmeath – progressing well, apparently. Pedigree cattle were next to get an airing: Belgian Blues. Then it was on to rare breeds of dog; she had a thing about Kerry Blues. He also learned that she had just started a postgraduate course in Medieval Literature.

Barry's mind was on other matters. Time was moving on. He looked at his watch a couple of times and Lena noticed he was getting restless.

"What's your hurry?"

"I'm expected back in London."

"Why so?"

"It's my girlfriend's birthday!"

"I hope you have a nice present for her."

"Of course."

"And flowers. You mustn't forget the flowers."

Lena volunteered to accompany him to the station. It was still raining. They walked and she talked. Hugs as they parted. Mission accomplished. Now there was light at the end of the tunnel. He had Ellie's party to look forward to.

In Irish the name 'McTaggart' means 'son of the priest'.

The Jobseeker

After his sudden departure from the job at London Bridge, Mark Jordan wasn't sure whether he or it would fall down first. Although the writing had been on the wall, the end was sudden.

"No point dwelling on it," he muttered to himself. "The building trade is nothing but a circus."

Mark next found his way to a house refurbishment in Chelsea. His sole task was to install a steel beam under the joists in the living room. That was all. They would pay him a week's wages irrespective of time taken.

Mark was there early, before eight. No one else appeared until nine.

"You're keen, aren't you?" said a tall guy with a nose ring and army jacket.

"It wouldn't look good to be late the first day," Mark replied.

When everyone had assembled, there were about a dozen men on the job. This crew consisted almost entirely of freaks, punks, old-age hippies, and new-age travellers. Mark found them to be a tightly knit group. As a team, they had worked together for years.

During the course of the morning, there were two long tea breaks. On both occasions, a teenager in a Crass hoodie was sent to McDonald's for refreshments.

"What d'you want?" he asked Mark before he went.

"Just a coffee."

"Only coffee? You'll starve."

Everyone was smoking hash, including the foreman.

"Mate, you want a pull?" he offered as a welcoming gesture.

Mark declined. "No thanks. It puts me to sleep."

"OK. Pass the duchy on the left-hand side," said a small wizened chippy, to roars of raucous laughter.

By lunchtime, the whole gang was stoned. Shortly afterwards, all hands went home. As the foreman said, "You couldn't be late twice in one day."

Mark realised the job could be done in a short time, probably in a couple of hours. While he wanted to get it over and done with, no one else seemed to be in any hurry.

"Two hours would do it," he remarked.

"Chill out, mate," said a guy with a Mohawk. "Rome wasn't built in a day."

Nothing here was straightforward. This team had its own modus operandi. Before the simplest task could be undertaken, a general meeting was called. The task was discussed at length by the whole crew. Then an action plan was agreed upon and eventually executed. It was very democratic.

The beam was outside. Such was its weight it would require the whole team to carry it in. Because he had a week to do the job, it didn't alarm Mark when the first day passed without any movement. The second day was much the same as the first. Inertia. In the morning, the foreman had received a letter from the neighbours complaining about litter. At break time, he proceeded to read it aloud to the crew as they dined on their burgers, fries, and milkshakes.

He finished dramatically: "And finally, unless the situation improves, we will have no recourse but to go to the Council."

He got up, slowly tore the letter into little bits, walked outside, and threw it into the neighbour's garden.

"Problem solved," he announced proudly.

Meanwhile, the beam remained outdoors. Mark was powerless. He leaned against a wall, cup of tea in hand, chatting with the electrician. This lad was a part-time DJ and had his own pirate radio station.

"So, how long you reckon before the beam moves?" Mark asked.

"Soon, soon," said the DJ-electrician. "We like to savour the moment. A bit of suspense."

On the third morning, there was a sudden burst of energy.

"Right lads, let's shift this beast!" someone cried.

The full team was mobilised, the beam brought in, and deposited in the middle of the living room.

Then it was time "to break for the burger," as the electrician described it.

An hour later, they hoisted the beam into place.

"Hold it there!" Mark barked. "She's level now and the height is perfect."

All he had to do was build in the two ends. By lunchtime, it was done.

"Great job. Cheers, mate," the foreman said, handing him his cash. "Safe travels."

Mark's hope was to find something long-term. He had seen an office block under construction in Colliers Wood, close to the Black Building. He went there that same afternoon. On arrival, he was directed to the foreman.

He walked in on a scene of utter chaos. Heaps of broken blocks and bricks were strewn all over the floor. The foreman was standing there right in the middle of it, surrounded by several brickies and a couple of wild-looking hod carriers. They were preparing to rebuild a wall which had recently been knocked down.

Terry, the foreman, was a tall, ruddy-faced man with glasses. He was covered in dust from head to foot.

"Are you taking on any bricklayers?" Mark enquired.

"When can you start?"

"As soon as you want."

"OK. Come in tomorrow. There is a good atmosphere on site. Everyone mucks in together."

A big hod carrier chipped in, "We like to have the craic here."

Next morning, Terry sent Mark to work with the hod carrier from the previous day.

"Al will show you where you're working. He'll keep you right."

Al was very helpful and was a hard worker. He was also permanently stoned. His knees and legs were covered in cuts. He kept falling through the scaffold while under the influence.

"Watch your step," Mark said, pulling him up for the third time.

"Cheers, mate," Al slurred. "Just a bit dizzy."

Other hod carriers were young and wild with it. Luke was seventeen and spoke of nothing but weed, drink, and court cases.

"Charged with GBH," he told Mark. "Solicitor reckons I'm going down for a spell."

A few days later, Luke decked Terry. Gone!

On Mark's section were two other bricklayers, Pete the Bodybuilder and Grumpy Gerry. Pete was a heavyset lad with a round face, a ponytail, and multiple piercings. He talked a lot about his diet.

"You really eat twenty-five raw eggs daily?" Mark asked.

"Every morning. Pure protein. Builds muscle," boasted Pete.

Gerry, a Sid James clone, grumbled constantly.

"This place is a bloody circus," he said. "Stoned brickies, brain-dead hoddies. No one knows what we're supposed to be doing. We're doomed."

"Are you always so cheerful?" Mark asked.

"I'm cheerful when I'm on my allotment," he snapped.

But even there, he was continually at war with birds, slugs, and other allotment owners. At home, Gerry's wife and son were a law unto themselves. They regularly left him to it and headed off on luxury holidays.

"I'll be with my sister for Christmas," he said. "At least she won't take the credit card."

As foreman, Terry was responsible for setting out the work. However, walls, windows, and doors had the uncanny knack of finding themselves in the wrong place. Bricklayers were constantly faced with irreconcilable discrepancies in levels, dimensions, and distances. Hence there were regular bouts of demolition. Terry was a legend among bricklayers, known far and wide as 'Take-it-down Terry.'

Terry presided over his band of mavericks in an aloof kind of way. He didn't like anyone bothering him with questions about work. His stock answer was "You wouldn't understand." The brickies worked away with the minimum of instruction or intervention.

Mark had seen the red flags early on. From bitter experience he knew where this was all heading. Whereas most of the lads accepted the chaos, he would sometimes ask for measurements. Terry saw him as a thorn in his side. It was only a matter of time before Mark was sacked. One day, Terry just blandly told him that there was no work left. In a way, Mark was relieved. He didn't want to be present when the sky fell in.

More than ever, Mark yearned for a period of stability. His next port of call was near Petticoat Lane.

When he started there, he was put working with an oddball. This lad owned his own house, lived alone, and led a Spartan lifestyle.

"One fork, one spoon, one plate, one bowl," the man boasted. "Saves on washing up."

"Yeah," said Mark. "Sounds like punishment to me."

Mark hadn't done his homework. Everything was built with 50 kilo blocks. When Mark saw them, he winced.

"I've got a dodgy back," he explained.

"Then you're in the wrong place, mate."

Time to move again.

Within a couple of days, he found work on a house refurbishment. To begin with, there was only himself and Archie, a potbellied Glaswegian with a whisky nose. Archie spent most of his time sweeping and tidying up. He was a dry kind of character and a Rangers man, a Hun.

"Peter owns the company," Archie said. "Most lads live round Angel. We drink in The Crown. You'll meet the foreman soon."

He loved to talk about the foreman in a reverential tone.

"The foreman is the son Peter never had."

"The foreman likes to keep the place clean."

"Wait till the foreman comes."

"What's this foreman like?" asked Mark.

"From Cavan."

"Oh God," Mark said. "Had a run-in with a Cavan man recently."

"Wait till I tell him that!"

Around midday, Mark noticed that Archie was starting to get restless. Soon afterwards, he disappeared. He didn't come back for an hour and a half. When he returned, it was obvious he was under the weather. He joked about "pints and pot noodles." Work was forgotten about.

The following morning, the foreman showed up. All round, a queer-looking fish, in a pair of striped shorts which were too tight for him. He wore a look of permanent anxiety.

Mark was beginning to have feelings of déjà vu. There wasn't much work being done. Archie and the foreman were as thick as thieves. At lunchtime they took off for the pub. Ninety minutes later they came back and had their pot noodles. That took another half hour. Just like the previous day, the rest of the afternoon was spent idling.

On the third morning, Mark was left waiting in the rain. The foreman and Archie didn't appear until nearly ten o'clock. As usual, they went off for their wet lunch. On their return, out of the blue, the foreman informed Mark that there was no more work.

"Sorry, Mark, Peter lost two contracts. You're done."

Mark stared. "You're joking?"

"I'm sorry. Not this time."

When presented with his wages, Mark knew it was for real.

Mark had long ago come to accept and absorb these shocks to the system.

But still. He was always hoping for something better.

He hurried off home in a daze, stopping only to buy an evening paper. He found another job almost immediately. It was a development of new houses in Putney.

His first contact there was with Dave the foreman. Mark took an instant dislike to him. The man was downright nasty, always scowling.

"You're with Barry," he said, pointing to a big bearded man. "Now get moving."

Barry, a big teddy bear of a man, grinned.

"Dave's a rough diamond. I have known him all my life. A hateful being. But he keeps the site running smoothly."

On his second week, Mark was sent to work with Paul, a thin-faced man from Swansea.

"Lost the lot in the divorce," Paul confided. "Now she's married a millionaire."

Paul was forever on the run from Social Security and the Child Support Agency.

After another few days, Mark's next partner was Graham, a bachelor from Yorkshire. He rented a bedsit in Balham not far from Mark. Graham had that flat, matter-of-fact tone of the Tyke. While mostly dour, at times he did manage the odd joke. Steve, their genial hod carrier, was the only person on site with the ability to humour him.

Steve was a dapper little grey-haired fellow in his forties. A rarity among building workers, he was extremely pleasant and mannerly. He saw everything in a humorous light and had his own unique way of going on:

"How's the rough gang getting on?"

"Are you all happy?"

"What can I get you?"

"Some Donald?" (Donald Duck was rhyming slang for muck/mortar).

Because Steve was so polite, everyone loved him. They joked that he was training to be a butler. Mark drove Steve home every evening, and they became known as the chauffeur and the butler.

While the job was well paid, the company wanted their pound of flesh. Dave ensured they got it. He didn't like to see anyone talking, never mind joking or laughing. All he wanted was heads down, bums up. He hadn't got his nickname, Dogsbreath, for nothing.

Once more, for Mark, the end came suddenly. Dave blamed him for something Graham had failed to do.

"That wasn't me," Mark argued.

"Gather up your tools. Your wages are in the office."

Mark decided to forget about work for the rest of the week. What was needed was some Real Ale Therapy. That evening he went to the Rose and Crown. As he walked in, he glimpsed a half-naked man at the bar, quietly drinking a pint. At closing time, the scantily dressed man was still there. This time Mark had a good look at him. He was wearing a nappy. Nothing else.

About right for the day that was in it!

Toothless in Tooting

For Peter Quinn, it was one of those watershed moments in time. Euro 2000 had finished the previous day. Not only that, but from an Irish perspective, motorcycling legend Joey Dunlop had been killed in an accident, and the latest edition of Drumcree had kicked off. All on the same day. Yet the world did not stop; life in London carried on. The tennis at Wimbledon was in full swing and was now nearing a conclusion.

His fast-approaching trip to Wales was a priority. There was an issue with his car. It had to be in rude health. After a long period of neglect, it was in dire need of a service. Maybe more. He had a feeling that a new timing belt might be required.

A colleague had recommended a garage not far from Jack Beard's pub in SW17. When Peter arrived there, he was interviewed by the chief mechanic. The man walked slowly round the car, pausing to kick each tyre as he passed. Then he asked if Peter could bring it back the next day. Peter explained that he needed the job done quickly. He was going away in the morning. Realising there would not be a next day, the mechanic backtracked. He said to leave the car and come back in two hours.

Now it struck Peter that he had no money on him. He figured that this guy was unlikely to deal in either cheques or cards. Cash was his only currency. He had two hours to kill anyway, so he set off to find an ATM.

He emerged from the garage deep in thought, the smell of oil and grease still following him. Suddenly, he became aware of a tall woman standing right in front of him. She wore a loose-fitting green coat over a yellow dress. Her greying hair was of medium length. Her face was turned away from him.

As he passed her, she turned towards him. Peter guessed she was in her forties. She looked straight at him and uttered something unintelligible. He was not sure if she was talking to herself or if the remark was addressed to him. Her clothes looked old-fashioned. She was very pale, and there was something about her eyes. Maybe the colour.

As he crossed the street, the lady followed him. She also seemed to quicken her step. As he moved ahead of her, she called out after him. He stopped and turned round to face her.

"Excuse me, sir."

"Yes!"

She smiled. Not warmly. Not coldly. Like a doll's smile.

"Can you help me?"

"I will if I can."

"Would you know of a good dentist in the area?"

Dentist? He had been wandering along with his head full of marching men, football, tennis, a dead biker, an unserviced car, and an ATM. Not to mention his upcoming trip to Wales. This question startled him from his reverie. It was a strange one. Her words were clear, with a faint echo, as if she were speaking from the far end of a long hallway. However, he paid less heed to this than to her accent. She was not English. Most likely German or Scandinavian.

"Are you German?"

"No, I'm Estonian. But you're right in one way. My ancestors were German. My name, Koch, is German. You're also not English?"

"No, I'm Irish. Coincidentally, I was just thinking of the Irish biker who lost his life in Tallinn."

"I don't follow the motor racing. It's very popular in Estonia. As for me, I love football. I follow Germany."

"They didn't do very well this time."

"Actually, I thought they were superb. Schuster and Rummenigge in particular. Allofs top-scored with three goals."

He thought those players were long retired but decided to be diplomatic.

"I'm sorry. I don't really follow soccer. I wouldn't know individual players. I believe the Portuguese team behaved badly."

"I didn't hear about that."

Following this sporting introduction, Peter explained that he himself was a stranger in these parts. He did not know the area, nor did he know any dentist. She was now walking alongside him and began to tell him about her teeth. There had been problems with several of them in the past. This had necessitated extractions, fillings, and root canal treatment.

She went on to describe how she used to suffer from very bad headaches after she had fillings. It was only on her last visit to the dentist that she discovered why. Previously, all her dentists had used fillings which included mercury. The last one had used mercury-free fillings. There were no headaches afterwards. Why didn't she go back there, he wondered.

Peter was not able to get a word in edgeways. She was talking so fast. She claimed that her teeth had rotted because she used to eat a lot of coconuts when she was young. Coconuts were very bad for the teeth. He had to believe her. This tale of the teeth was making him feel uneasy. He was now walking faster. She had also accelerated to keep pace with him. And the faster she walked, the faster her words came out.

"Why didn't you go back to the last dentist?"

"But the last dentist was in Estonia."

"You have no plans to return there soon?"

"No, it would be too expensive to travel there. I have no family there any more anyway."

"I see."

"Actually, I had a very good relationship with that dentist. She was Hungarian. I always felt so relaxed in her surgery. Largely thanks to her big ginger cat. He would often come and sit on my knee during treatment. A great distraction."

As they passed a bench, the lady halted.

"I need to sit down for a few minutes. Will you join me?"

Peter wondered why. She did not look tired. In fact, he struggled to keep up with her. She seemed to just glide along.

"Okay. I guess a rest will do no harm."

Then he understood. She had a cigarette in her hand.

He was still thinking of the dentist's cat in Tallinn. Not something one would encounter in these parts. Dentists' cats usually stayed out of sight. Health and safety would forbid it, surely. However, the mention of Estonia and cats brought back a memory. He told her he had been to the Baltic states before and went on to tell her about an experience with cats in that part of the world.

"I was visiting a friend. It was a Sunday morning and we had taken the ferry from Tallinn to Helsinki. At the harbour in Helsinki was a fish market. As we walked through the market, we saw a crowd. It was a kind of cat circus. In charge of this operation was a blonde 'ringmistress.' She stood out with her red blouse, black skirt, and knee-high black boots. The supporting cast included two young girls, a white poodle, and two cats."

"I have heard of that lady and her cats. She is Russian and is very famous in Finland."

She kept edging closer to him as she talked. The smile never wavered, never twitched. She was making him nervous the way she looked at him. Her eyes were focused on him, always a little to the left, as if she were looking over his shoulder. He had been trying to figure out what it was with her eye colour. They seemed to change from grey, to green, to blue. She still had a cigarette in her hand, but he never saw her put it to her mouth.

As they walked along, he paused periodically to check the street names. When he stopped, she stopped.

"I'm looking for an ATM."

In a quick riposte, she said, "I have spent many years looking for something. My problem is that I don't know what it is."

He could not help but laugh inwardly at this remark. He diplomatically agreed.

"That can happen. Perhaps you're looking too hard. If you forget about it for a while, it might just appear in front of you."

He changed tack.

"Have you heard about the new TV show, Big Brother?"

"I'm sorry. I haven't."

"I'm looking forward to the first episode on Friday night."

When he saw she did not have much interest in reality TV, he switched back to sport.

"I suppose you'll miss the football now it's over."

"It has left a gap in my life. What will we do now for the rest of the year?"

Having detailed her highs and lows during the competition, she admitted to having drunk too much. She leaned towards Peter and whispered that she had consumed a bottle of wine every night. Then, as an afterthought, she added that, in a way, she was glad it was over. That amount of drinking could not go on. She was determined there would be no repeat.

She kept saying she needed to cross the road but did not. He wished she would. Instead, she kept walking alongside him. Once more Peter stopped to take his bearings as he searched for the ATM. He had got vague directions from the mechanic. He figured he still had some distance to go. When he turned round, the lady had gone. Not a sign of her. He was surprised but relieved.

His head was spinning. So many random, disjointed thoughts. He found himself on the way back to the garage with no recollection of having been to the bank at all. When he arrived, the car was sitting outside, a sign that it was ready.

On arrival, the mechanic informed him that his timing belt would last another while. He invited Peter to check the car over and then presented him with the bill.

Peter wondered if the mechanic might know the lady he had encountered earlier.

"Sorry, but can I ask you a question? Nothing at all to do with cars."

"Go on."

"It's about a lady I saw earlier."

The man smiled knowingly. "Tell me more."

Peter took a deep breath, gathering his thoughts as he looked at the mechanic. "She had a green coat, yellow dress, and was speaking unusually fast. I think she mentioned being Estonian."

"Yes, I know."

"I just felt there was something not right about her."

"Her name is Liisa. Quite a character, isn't she? Loves to share her stories, but they can be a bit... peculiar."

"Peculiar how?" Peter questioned, curiosity piqued.

"She often talks about her life back in Estonia, her relationship with cats, and a host of other random topics. Sometimes it's like she's in her own world."

"So, she's not... dangerous or anything?"

"No, not at all dangerous. She died 20 years ago."

Peter gasped. The mechanic's words were left hanging in the air. "She died 20 years ago."

For a moment, he thought he had misheard. But the man's expression was deadly serious, his eyes steady.

"What?" Peter managed, his voice no more than a whisper.

"Liisa Koch. Used to live around here. Estonian woman, always wore that green coat. Died in 1980."

"But she was obsessed with dentists. Why?"

He beckoned Peter to follow him.

"See that boarded-up building across the road? Used to be a dental surgery. Closed down after... well." He lowered his voice. "After her."

Peter's breath hitched. "What happened?"

"She was their last patient. Had a bad reaction to anaesthetic, just never woke up. Place shut down within a week."

He wiped his hands on a rag. "Several people have seen her. Always asking about dentists. Always complaining about her teeth."

Peter climbed into his car and started the engine. As he was about to pull away, he caught a flicker of movement in the rear-view mirror.

A woman in a green coat.

Standing by the road.

Cigarette in hand.

Smiling that doll-like smile.

Lady Luck

Walter Walsh had been in London for two years. He was thirty-eight, single, and looking for love. So far, his search had proved fruitless. Love didn't seem to be looking for him. Yet optimism prevailed. He kept telling himself that he only had to get lucky once.

At weekends, he would go to Irish pubs and clubs. Most of the ladies who frequented these places had been around the block. They didn't converse; they conducted interviews. No answer satisfied their curiosity. They weren't going to be fooled by anyone.

"What brought you to London?"

"Are you wanted in Ireland?"

"Where's your wife?"

"How do I know you're not lying?"

He had also tried his hand at online dating. While there appeared to be a good number of ladies to choose from, that too had been a disappointment. Of the ladies he did meet, some exaggerated their beauty and some underestimated their age. Others just wanted to chat online. They didn't want to meet anyone in person. Time wasters and tyre kickers aplenty.

He should have known better than to meet those with handles like #Jellybelly and #Sparetyre. But he was new to all this. It was a learning curve. He did get mildly excited at the prospect of meeting #Thundertits. However, when it came to a face-to-face encounter, she reneged. He consoled himself with the thought that she was probably a dowdy, middle-aged, cat-owning spinster who played bingo five nights a week.

After a month, he cancelled his subscription. There had been no close encounters of any kind. One of his friends had met his partner using the small ads of a local newspaper. He suggested that Walter give that a try.

"Why not?" thought Walter.

"Have you ever considered an Oriental lady?" asked his friend.

"No, that thought hadn't occurred to me."

"Well, as you know, it worked for me."

"Can you help me get set up?"

"Of course."

Thus, Walter came to place an ad specifically seeking an Asian female.

The first reply he received was from a Fijian air hostess. After a few texts, they spoke on the phone.

"Hi, this is Walter. Nice to finally get to talk."

"Hi Walter. I'm Marianne from Fiji."

"I'm from Ireland."

"Really! My best friend is from Ireland. We work together."

"Are you with British Airways?"

"No, Virgin Atlantic."

"What do you like to do in your free time?"

"I love line dancing. That's my passion. And you?"

"I'm into sports. I follow Arsenal. There's a strong Irish connection."

"I guess you don't work regular hours?"

"You're right. But I have this coming weekend off."

"Maybe we can meet?"

"Yes, why not? What with my best friend being Irish, I couldn't refuse you."

For Walter, that was good enough to be getting on with.

They met at a tube station near Heathrow on Saturday afternoon. Marianne brought him to a local pub.

"Did you ever go line dancing?" Marianne queried.

"Not yet," replied Walter.

"When I am off, I go as often as I can. My friend Veronica is also a keen dancer. The beauty of our work is that we work together and are off together."

"I didn't know line dancing was popular here."

"There are several venues around London. We go to a place in Chiswick."

Walter was invited to view some pictures of her in action. There wasn't much he could say. He knew nothing about line dancing but pretended to be very impressed.

"Are you hungry?" enquired Marianne. "I know a good steakhouse. It is within walking distance."

Walter wasn't desperately hungry. Before he had time to respond, she had finished her drink and put on her coat. They were there in no time. Drinks were ordered. They then focused on the food. The lady made sure to sample the full menu. They had starters, steaks, and sweets. Marianne was ravenous. She devoured everything in front of her. The wine flowed and, for a time, the conversation flowed. Time passed quickly.

When all the food and wine had been consumed, things took an unexpected turn.

"I think I've twisted my ankle again," moaned Marianne.

"What happened?"

"It's an old injury. The pain is terrible."

"Can I do anything to help?"

"No. I'll have to go home. I'm sorry."

"No need to apologise."

"I'll call you soon."

Walter watched her hobble off, leaving him alone with his doubts and a hefty bill.

Walter's next date was with a pretty Indian divorcee. They met in a pub on Clapham Common. This lady was very pleasant but, all the while they were together, she kept wondering out loud if she would prefer someone younger. After debating with herself for a couple of hours, she went off home. Walter didn't even get her name, but she too promised to ring soon. Again, he had a grave suspicion, even a premonition, that the call would never come.

Then came Mary, a widow from Hayes, Middlesex. She invited Walter out there to meet her. He had never been to Hayes but discovered it was north of Heathrow Airport. EMI once had a factory there producing vinyl records. The Beatles had even visited it back in the day.

Walter was issued with instructions on how to get there by train. Mary would be waiting in the station car park. He was to look out for a little lady in a red jeep. On arrival, Walter spotted the jeep immediately and Mary beckoned him to get in. She drove to a pub where they had lunch. This was followed by a leisurely walk round the town.

Mary talked as they walked. She had had a traumatic experience and was extremely cautious regarding relationships. Following the death of her husband, she had been comforted by his best friend. However, the grieving Mary soon realised the man wanted something more than friendship. She didn't. Her "comforter" ended up stalking her, which added to her grief. It got so bad she eventually had to move house.

Having got this weight off her chest, Mary decided it was time to drive Walter back to the station. She promised to ring him. Again, he didn't hold out any great expectations. Indeed, there was no call, but the next day he did receive an email. On mature reflection, Mary had decided not to progress the relationship.

Walter saw no point in soul-searching. He kept going, buoyed up by his mantra.

He only needed to get lucky once.

His next encounter was with a separated lady from Mauritius. She was a nursing sister in a local hospital. They met in Tooting Broadway and retired to a pub for refreshments, this after she had declared she didn't like pubs and hated smoking.

The lady seemed to be nervous, even fearful, and certainly distracted. Walter had a strong suspicion that this was the first time she had been on a blind date. There was no settling her. She had just begun to tell him about her family when she abruptly announced she had to go. It was time to pick up her daughter from a music lesson. She promised to call Walter and tell him more. Déjà vu. Another polite goodbye. "Don't call me, I'll call you!"

Walter had now gone through the list of potential matches. The dates had dried up. It was time to reflect. Was there something about him that was unattractive to the Asian ladies? Did he lack empathy? Did they expect more comment from him? Should he have come bearing gifts? Had he disrespected their culture in some unknown way? He didn't know. How could he?

For two weeks there was no activity at all. Then, out of the blue, he received a voice message. This person began by stating:

"I know I'm not Asian and I am older than you. You'd hardly be interested in me, but I'm contacting you anyway."

The lady went on to declare that she owned her own house and was on the lookout for a man. Walter wasn't sure what to make of her. She seemed to be all over the place. After listening to the message again, he decided he would ring her back, for better or worse.

When he rang, Walter was greeted by the lady who introduced herself as Alice. She repeated what she'd said in the voice message.

"Though I am older than you, I am youthful looking."

Be that as it may, Walter knew she didn't meet any of his specifications or expectations. He had a sinking feeling but did nothing to call a halt. At that moment, he didn't have many options.

"Where do you live?" she queried.

"I'm in Tooting."

"Not too far away. I'm in Surbiton. I can drive up."

"When?"

"I should be there in an hour."

When he didn't reply immediately she continued, "I'll ring you when I'm near. Look out for a blue Fiesta."

About an hour later came the call. Walter said he would meet her outside a nearby pub. As the Fiesta pulled up, he could see that Alice had at least twenty years on him. Yet he got in beside her, unsure whether it was voluntary or involuntary.

"Where would you like to go, Alice?"

"I don't like pubs. Maybe a coffee shop."

She talked away as they drove towards Wandsworth. Eventually, she parked outside a Pizza Hut. In they went.

They ordered coffee, which was served in two large mugs. When the drinks came, the old dear had to use both hands to get the vessel to her lips. Then she started on her life story. It was largely about the men in her life. She was a little bit muddled and sometimes Walter too was confused as she moved back and forth between lovers. He found his mind wandering. How had he got himself into this tangle?

"My last partner was a builder. Initially, I met this man in a park on the banks of the Thames. He parked beside me and we got talking. All went well for several weeks. Until the day he was to move in."

"What happened?"

"He rode off on his motorbike that morning. I haven't seen him since."

The tears flowed down her cheeks. Clearly, she hadn't seen it coming. As she was catching her breath, she ventured, "Now Walter, tell me about you." Just as he was about to open his mouth, she started again. She continued the tale of the biker. She knew where he lived and had driven past his house on several occasions. However, she hadn't the courage to go up to the door. She had phoned a few times as well, but he never answered.

Again she asked about Walter's life but, before he had time to reply, she launched into an account of the second-last man.

"Before I met Winston, I lived with another man for eleven years. He left me for another woman, a neighbour."

"That must have been hard to take!"

"Yes. Especially as the lady is very loud, overweight, and has several brats. I just don't know what he sees in her."

"There's no accounting for taste!"

Then she leaned over and whispered.

"He still rings me regularly to check if I'm all right. He even calls to see me. Sometimes we have a wee canoodle."

As the hours passed, it evolved into a saga. Walter, the silenced witness, had long finished his second coffee. It was tedious. He wanted out. Shock tactics were called for. He suggested they could spend the rest of the afternoon in bed.

"I couldn't do that after just meeting someone," she said without a hint of surprise.

She was neither shaken nor stirred. She just continued to lament.

Alice had alluded to her son in passing, as well as her brother. She lamented that her life had been so humdrum while her brother had had such a colourful and eventful career. Then came a bolt from the blue.

"In my younger days, I was a DJ. I was raped by a Jamaican DJ. That's how my son came about."

She wondered if it was her fault for going back to his place.

"Did I lead him on?" she asked.

Walter was used to being asked tricky questions, but he had no oven-ready answer to that one.

Eventually, Alice paused. She looked at her watch and realised hours had passed. Time to be getting home. As they drove back, she started to rehash the whole story. Even after the car stopped, she kept talking. Again, Walter went for the nuclear option and asked for sex. Again she refused, but she said she felt guilty. However, it did break up her flow. And as she hesitated, Walter made off.

All things considered, it could have been worse.

She could have said "YES!"

For once, he had got lucky. Just not in the manner intended.

The Wandering Minstrel

Neither of them paid much heed when they first saw the figure in the distance. She was preoccupied with the needs of her granddaughter. He was ruminating on the meal he had enjoyed earlier.

She had volunteered to walk him to the station. He was quite sure he could find his way. Even though it was a damp November evening, she insisted. She feared he might get lost.

"The company will shorten the walk! Anyway, the child needs some fresh air."

In the twilight they could see the distant body coming their way. Impossible to know who or what it was, man or beast? Whatever it was, it had an odd shape and a peculiar gait. Everything about it looked out of sync.

They were walking down a long, dimly lit alley. As the figure approached, Lena became apprehensive.

"What is it, Barry? The baby!"

"Don't worry. It's just a man carrying some heavy goods."

As the wayfarer approached, they could see he was small in stature and weighed down with very bulky items. What looked like a large musical instrument was slung over his shoulder. One hand held it in position. The other hand held two heavy carrier bags, giving him a kind of false equilibrium.

The man came up to them, stopped, and lowered his burden. A tin of cat food fell from a bag. Lena picked it up and handed it to him. As he put it back in the bag, he looked pleadingly into her face. She quickly sized up the situation. Plainly, this poor fellow was disoriented. Lost.

"Are you OK, sir? You look exhausted!"

"I'm a little tired, that's all."

"Have you far to go?"

"Actually, I'm on my way to the station."

"Well, if that's the case, you're headed in the wrong direction."

The traveller realigned himself. Lena tried to give him directions, but she wasn't sure he was listening. Then she had a brainwave. Pointing to Barry, she declared,

"My nephew is going there too. You can go together."

"Thanks for everything, dear, especially the lunch."

"Will you be okay, Barry? If you're feeling lonely, just call. Come and see us soon."

"Don't worry, I'll be fine."

"There's a race meeting early next month. You might like that!"

"Yes, that's an idea! I do like a punt."

Barry bent down to have a last look at the child struggling in the buggy. It kicked off its blanket and began to whimper. This was Lena's cue to depart the scene. She executed a swift three-point turn and waved as she hurried off.

It now dawned on a bemused Barry that he had been left in charge of a helpless, hapless, lost little man. Totally bizarre. Just the look of this poor creature, the set of him, dwarfed by his burden. What had brought him here anyway?

Barry felt tired. It had been a long day. He had spent a good part of the morning on tubes, trains, and taxis. Then he'd eaten a big lunch. Now it all had to be done again in reverse order. This time he also had to ensure this stranger made it safely to the station. He hardly knew the way himself, and there was the small matter of Ellie's birthday party later on.

The duo stood silently in the gloom. While Barry was young, fit, and fresh-faced, his travelling companion was a little older, overweight, and out of shape.

One seemed to be waiting for the other to speak. Finally, the smaller of the two spoke in a low voice.

"Hi, I'm Edward."

"Hi, Edward. I'm Barry."

"I don't want to miss my train! Ginger will be waiting for me."

"Don't worry. We'll not be long. I don't want to miss it either. My girlfriend is 24 today."

Without further ado, Barry led the way as they set off for the station. One looking forward to a birthday bash, the other to being reunited with his cat. As they proceeded, Barry attempted to evaluate this new man in his life. Most likely a bachelor. At a guess, probably in his late thirties.

Bespectacled. Slightly hunched. A result of his unwieldy load?

Edward was soon puffing and panting. He kept dropping back, further irritating his reluctant escort. Hardly able to put one foot past the other, he looked on the brink of collapse. Finally, he came to a halt.

"It's my cello," he said breathlessly as he set the instrument on the ground.

"I was thinking that!" replied Barry drily.

Again Barry scrutinised the small stranger and his not-so-small burden. Edward wasn't going to make it. Barry had to act. If they were ever going to reach the station, he had to take charge of the cello. Edward protested, but in the end, he meekly handed it over.

Nonchalantly, Barry attempted to sling the cello onto his shoulder. He almost lost his balance as it slid off. The weight of it. He did manage to secure it at the second attempt. Now he understood Edward's posture, or lack of it.

Even minus his instrument, the bags were still a strain on the diminutive musician. Nor did the load-sharing speed them up greatly. However, they eventually did reach the station. Barry was relieved. Mission accomplished. Now all he wanted was to get on the train, chill out, and maybe even have a nap.

"Thank you, Barry. I would never have made it without you."

"Don't mention it. It's been a pleasure."

"Where are you travelling to?"

"Kings Cross."

"Me too. Let's go together!"

"Why not?" sighed Barry.

In the light of the station, Barry got his first clear view of the wandering minstrel. He was indeed a queer-looking little fish. The small body topped with a big head. Glasses perched on a snub nose. Two big green eyes constantly blinking behind thick lenses.

The cello was almost as tall as its owner. Looking now at man and instrument together, Barry was still baffled. How had Edward managed to carry his load as far as he did? The impossibility and absurdity of the whole situation.

They made their way to Platform 1. There was still plenty of time. Edward immediately sought out a bench. They sat for some time without speaking.

Eventually, Barry broke the silence.

"So you have a cat?"

"Indeed I do. So precious to me, but so fussy."

"Why so?"

"Well, for a start, she will only eat one type of cat food."

Barry had already seen the evidence. It was the brand which 90% of the cat population preferred.

All the while the moggy master was rummaging around in the other bag. He produced a carton of milk, opened it, and gulped down a few lengthy draughts.

"Feeling better after that?" commented Barry.

"Yes, it gives me energy. I like the full fat, but I also had to buy some semi-skimmed for my friend. She is a little overweight."

Barry was beginning to see how finicky the cat was. However, he did find it a little peculiar that a marmalade cat should be on a weight reduction plan or drinking milk of any sort. Weren't most cats lactose intolerant?

Barry went off to buy some water. On his return, the cellist confided that he was on his way home to Whitechapel. He was coming from his music class. Barry was only half listening. His mind was on other matters. He was thinking of Ellie's birthday party.

"We fight over our favourite armchair. Who gets there first. Once she's settled there, she can't be moved. I say 'she' but to be honest I have no idea what sex it is."

There was a long pause. Barry, who had been lost in thought, suddenly realised that he was expected to respond.

Barry had zero credentials as a cat sexer, but now he was being called on to determine whether the cat was a Tom or a Molly. At least Ginger was a suitably gender-neutral name. Diplomatically, albeit vaguely, he tried to explain the differences in feline genitalia. He advised on how these might be examined, without upsetting the animal.

When the train came, Barry carried the cello on board. One seat in their compartment was already occupied by an ancient hippie. Just as the two newcomers had made themselves comfortable, a young lady entered and sat next to Barry. She was followed soon after by a portly middle-aged woman who decided to sit down beside the old-age traveller.

As the lady was in the process of taking her seat, there was an almighty howl. A dog shot out from under her. Pandemonium broke out. The lady screamed. Then both ladies screamed in harmony as the mutt raced round the carriage on three legs, yelping for all it was worth. Eventually, it jumped into the loving arms of its owner.

The woman stood there, transfixed. She had gone pale and looked ready to faint. Barry came to the rescue and helped her to another seat, away from the dog and its owner. He handed her his unopened bottle of water.

The still-whining Fido crawled in between its master and the cellist. Edward never batted an eyelid. He began to speak quietly to the hound and managed to calm it down. Barry was impressed. Edward might not know a lot about cats, but he had a way with dogs. A dog whisperer?

The dog owner apologised to the lady and thanked Edward.

Barry also congratulated Edward. "You did a great job calming the dog."

"Oh, I used to have a dog, but when Ginger came along, things changed. Unfortunately, it had to go. They simply couldn't co-exist."

After hearing Barry's accent, the younger lady struck up a conversation with him. She talked of her Irish mother's love of animals. Their chat was continually interrupted by phone calls from her boyfriend. A rendezvous was being planned. Finally, she got off at Potters Bar. Edward then resumed on the topic of Grimalkin.

The cellist had many concerns about the cat, especially around it having kittens.

"How would I even know if it gave birth? How would I find the offspring?"

Barry wasn't totally prepared for his revised role of agony cat uncle.

"You should watch it carefully for changes in behaviour. When a cat has kittens, it hides them for several weeks. That's of course assuming that it is a Molly. Have you never had a cat before?"

"We did have an old cat years ago. I think it was a Tom. It never had kittens."

"Did you not help to look after it?"

"No, my mother looked after it. It was her pet. I took nothing to do with it."

He then went on to describe his present cat.

"It seems to be left-handed."

"A southpaw," suggested Barry mischievously.

Barry was growing into his role as a cat behaviourist.

"Cats can favour either paw or even be ambidextrous," he asserted.

"Would this be any indication of its sex?"

"Not really," said Barry, dismissing this idea with a shake of his head.

Edward's excitement grew as they approached London.

"I'm relieved that the train is on time. I don't like being away from Ginger."

"You seem to have a very strong bond."

"Of course. A shared passion for music. She loves to hear me play *Le Cygne*."

Barry decided he might as well humour Edward. "She must have a musical ear?"

"Sometimes she sings along!" replied Edward matter-of-factly.

Barry was flummoxed. But hadn't he asked for it?

A singing cat indeed. And probably attending Weight Watchers.

He sat there dumbstruck. Anyway, they were nearly there now. He just wasn't willing or able to go any further down this rabbit hole. He just wanted to get home to Ellie.

Barry felt relief as the train pulled into Kings Cross. He had done more than his duty for one day, guiding a lost soul to his destination. He helped Edward to disembark. They stood on the crowded platform ready to bid farewell, for the second time that evening.

Just as they were about to part, a buxom redhead emerged from the throng. She promptly threw her arms around the cellist and hugged him.

"So my little music man is back. How was your lesson, Eddie?"

"It was wonderful, darling. Say hello to Barry. He has been such a help to me."

"Hello Barry, I'm Ginger! Thanks ever so much. I was so worried that Eddie might get lost. Now if you will excuse us, we've got to go. Max is home alone."

"I'm in a hurry myself. It's my girlfriend's birthday," shouted Barry over his shoulder as he rushed off.

Part Two

Pearl River Lessons

The Xmas Party

It was only the beginning of November, but GWE (Great Wall English) were having their Christmas party.

"A bit early for this, isn't it?" Joe McKenna muttered to no one in particular.

"This is China," came the chorus of replies — the standard response to anything that defied logic.

There was a buzz of excitement in the teachers' room. Chinese staff had been looking forward to this night for weeks. Even the students picked up on the festive mood. Work was a breeze that day. As an added bonus, Ronnie, the manager, was absent. So too was his deputy, Sunny.

"Funny how those two always disappear at the same time," McKenna remarked, sparking laughter all round.

Alex, the Chinese-American teacher, smirked. "You think that's a coincidence? And where's Fat Freddy? Bet he's lurking somewhere, watching them!"

"Freddy? Spying on Ronnie and Sunny?" McKenna scowled. "They never go anywhere together. They avoid each other like the plague. And Freddy wouldn't be caught dead with either of them."

The tall, bald, bespectacled Ronnie saw himself as a cultured individual and was known to sometimes play the violin in the centre. He had been nicknamed Captain Mainwaring, a snobbish and pompous character from a

British sitcom. At times he suffered from gout, which tended to affect his humour.

Sunny was a mild-mannered individual, popular with teachers and students alike. She was an only child and had the responsibility of supporting the whole family. Her father was disabled and her mother his carer. Despite her situation, she always had a smile for everyone.

"You know what's really going on?" Alex grinned. "Freddy's not just watching — he's part of a threesome with them."

"Get out," McKenna laughed. "Freddy's probably in some gaming arcade, playing the claw machine."

McKenna was aware of Freddy's hobby and also knew he had amassed a large number of soft toys from this pastime.

All classes were finished by 7.00 p.m. and McKenna went home in a taxi. His flatmate Jimmy and a group of Chinese friends were busy playing cards and drinking beer. He let Jimmy know that Denis, his Irish friend, might be staying over. Jimmy was tired of seeing Denis but said nothing. McKenna dropped off his backpack and walked to the party venue, which was just around the corner.

When he arrived at the party, there were quite a few people already there. He soon spotted Denis away in a far corner. He was in deep conversation with a group of teachers who weren't known to McKenna. His other Irish friend, Charlie, was there too. Charlie was involved in an intense discussion with a group of ladies. Soon after, the whole group moved off out of sight.

Charlie was a rough-and-ready character. He always stood out with his fuzzy grey hair and his thick jam-jar glasses. In his time, he had been a festival and concert promoter, rapper and, more recently, a movie maker.

Denis was a more refined type. He always dressed well and was a sports fanatic. In his youth, he had been a promising soccer player, but injury had cut short his career. After that, he had spent his time in sports-related work and study. McKenna hadn't known either of them very long, but he did know Charlie had a Jekyll-and-Hyde personality; he changed totally when he drank alcohol. He also had a great dislike of Scotsmen.

After a while, everyone was given the signal that they could start to eat. It was a self-service buffet. There was a huge spread — every type of food you could possibly imagine. McKenna had two big plates of food and drank two pints of Carlsberg. He then had a couple of glasses of fruit juice before going back on the beer again.

"Alex, you're gonna explode," McKenna said, watching his friend tucking into his third plate.

"Well worth it, Joe," Alex mumbled through a mouthful of noodles.

Nearby, Fat Freddy rubbed his belly. "There's this girl in my building, got a boyfriend, but he's a skinny little thing. She loves my gifts."

Freddy was bombarding the girl with dolls and stuffed animals from his hoard as he tried to prise her away from her boyfriend.

"What a smooth operator," McKenna drawled sardonically.

A Canadian teacher known as Professor Sylvester sat at one end of the table surrounded by a group of Chinese teachers. He was well-known for playing the stock exchange and also for his English Corners on off-the-wall topics. On this occasion, he was pontificating on global warming and the threat to the caribou on the tundra.

"Anyone actually following this?" one teacher whispered.

"Not a clue," admitted another.

Teachers from various centres passed back and forth. Some McKenna knew and some he didn't. Alex and he were reunited with their old friend Martha. The three of them had trained together. Martha was now working in Panyu, a distant suburb.

"How's life in Panyu?" enquired McKenna.

"It's fine, I'm enjoying it. Staff and students are very friendly."

"I heard they eat dogs down there," chipped in Alex mischievously.

Martha laughed. "Yes, that's right. I have seen it served in several restaurants."

Alex was persistent. "Have you tried it?"

"No, of course not. I'm American, in case you forgot, Alex."

McKenna laughed. That was Alex told off.

McKenna was on his way to the bar when he heard that Charlie had been acting up.

"Oh no," he thought, "he's at it already!"

He hadn't expected this so early in the evening. There would be no peace this night. The bold Charlie had been asking people if they wanted to fight. Luckily, the offended parties had refused to engage. One of them was a young teacher who had just arrived in town that very day. Charlie had called him "a haggis-eating Scottish bastard." What an introduction to China!

Those who had witnessed these incidents were shocked. They had only ever encountered a very pleasant, mild-mannered Charlie. They had never seen him on the rampage.

"You know Charlie's a Jekyll-and-Hyde character," McKenna warned a group of teachers who stood open-mouthed. "A lovely man sober, a menace drunk."

One Irish teacher took it on herself to give Charlie a severe reprimand.

"You're a disgrace to Ireland! Embarrassing the whole country!"

Charlie grinned. "Ah, lighten up."

She might as well not have bothered. Charlie was beyond recall.

Denis had missed that episode but had a sense of foreboding. He had heard that Charlie had arrived at the venue in mid-afternoon and had been drinking ever since. He sought out McKenna, who updated him on Charlie's activities. Both knew there was likely to be further mayhem before very long. This drunken Charlie was a ticking time bomb. They also knew there was very little they could do to prevent it.

McKenna was back and forth to his table. Despite the temptation of so much food, he couldn't eat any more. He was distracted. Alex, who had about half McKenna's body mass, kept eating.

Over the course of the evening, the study assistants spent their time listening and watching, taking it all in. This was a special night for them. Having eaten and drunk to their hearts' content, most of them left to catch the last metro. A few hugged their favourite teachers as they made their way out.

Charlie went on to meet a teacher from Birmingham during the course of the evening. Like Charlie, this new friend was also a musician. This led to talk of forming a band. Denis thought this might distract Charlie for a while and keep him out of trouble. McKenna had his doubts.

During a lull in proceedings, Denis had thoughts of going home. He was staying with Charlie.

"Can you give me a key, Charlie? I'm tired and want to go home."

Charlie was still deeply engaged in the talks on band formation.

Eventually he heard Denis. "I don't have a key on me."

Then Denis, as expected, turned to McKenna.

"Can I sleep at your place again tonight, Joe?" (He had stayed the night before.)

McKenna agreed. "No problem, as long as you don't mind Jimmy's friends. They could be there till all hours playing cards."

"I don't mind at all. I might even join them," said Denis with a wide grin on his face.

Having concluded the talks on band formation, Charlie approached Huey, the visiting Head of Marketing from Shanghai. Huey was a very dour, no-nonsense kind of Chinese businessman — small, stout, and bespectacled. A little bulldog of a man.

"Give us a hug!" Charlie slurred, planting a sloppy kiss on Huey's cheek.

Huey shoved him off, disgusted. "This is unacceptable! I will be reporting you to your manager first thing Monday morning."

It didn't discourage the bold Charlie. He was on a roll. Moments later, he challenged another Scottish teacher to a fight.

Kevin, the Irish-American Regional Manager, was presiding over the whole affair. Dressed very casually, he mingled easily with all and sundry. During the evening, he organised a raffle, made a few draws and awarded prizes to various people. He later moved everyone into a big room where he kept buying drinks. On several occasions he came with a bucketful of bottles and dumped them out on a table to slake the thirst of the waiting teachers. Mainwaring was at his most pompous, motoring round the place preaching to anyone who would listen. He was drinking bottles of Erdinger and, surprisingly, he too was buying drinks for all comers.

Charlie kept drinking and was becoming more and more erratic. His friends were trying to keep an eye on him at this stage, mainly to make sure he didn't harm himself. At one point, he walked out into a corridor empty-handed and came back with a full bottle of Erdinger. They couldn't figure out where he had found it. There was no bar out there. Probably stole it off Mainwaring!

Mainwaring suspected Charlie of the beer theft. He couldn't prove it, but he was fuming. Not just about the beer, but for his series of offences during the evening. It was a perfect opportunity to get on his high horse.

"This behaviour is an outrage! This man has damaged the good name of GWE. He will have to be held to account," he ranted.

"The gout must be at him," McKenna muttered to himself.

By now everyone was well on. No one else paid the slightest attention.

Charlie had meanwhile engaged with the people at another table. The unwary listeners weren't prepared for his rant about the cartoon character Mickey Mouse. Charlie was infatuated with the American rodent. Here he was describing his upcoming movie featuring Mickey. To the uninitiated, this always sounded like fun as he described his plans for the real Mickey and a cast of fake

Mickeys including the Irish Mícheál O'Muis and a host of other international Mickeys.

Those who knew him had heard about this movie many times before and were tired of listening to his diatribe. Denis and McKenna decided it was as good a time as any to slip away. They didn't tell Charlie they were going. He was so engrossed he never even noticed. Denis had a feeling he was without money, keys or phone.

When they got back to the apartment, Jimmy was there alone. The card players had gone. Jimmy had a bed ready for Denis, but first he made tea for the three of them. He wanted to hear about the party, and especially Charlie. As they drank their tea, McKenna updated Jimmy on Charlie's antics. Denis watched a drug deal unfolding on the street down below. They finished the tea and went to bed.

Over the weekend, there was more news about the party. At the end of the night, Charlie had abused a barman and refused to pay for a number of drinks. Mainwaring was the only other person still there, and he got saddled with the bill. Not only that, but he had to send the drunken Charlie home in a taxi and pay the fare.

By Monday, Rex, Charlie's manager, had been alerted. Huey, the marketing man, had been on to him. A Scottish teacher had also submitted a complaint. Charlie was in hot water. Rex wanted Charlie fired. Mainwaring wanted Charlie fired. They claimed that Charlie's behaviour was totally at odds with the ethos of GWE. It was now all down to Kevin, the Regional Manager.

Charlie was summoned to a meeting at Head Office. His fate looked certain. His defence was that all these incidents happened outside the workplace. He had always behaved properly at work and was popular with students and colleagues. Somehow, he managed to wriggle out of it. He escaped with a written warning. Mainwaring and Rex were outraged, but Kevin just passed it off.

"Sure I've two old uncles in Ireland who are ten times worse."

"Lucky boy," said McKenna when he heard.

Denis just shook his head. "He'll do it again, Joe."

"That's for sure, Denis," McKenna agreed.

And so Charlie lived to "fight" another day.

Great Wall English

It was April 2012, and Joe McKenna was emigrating for the third time in his career. He needed a fresh challenge. As he saw it, Ireland had run out of ideas. He was headed to China to teach at Great Wall English (GWE).

The company had agreed to put him up in a hotel for a week. After that, he was responsible for his own accommodation. On the second day there, he was in his room when a knock came at the door.

"Mr McKenna? I'm Ronnie, your new boss." A tall, stern-faced man extended a hand. "Ready to see your new workplace?"

McKenna forced a smile. "Yes. Thank you."

When they arrived, Sunny, the Assistant Manager, was there to greet them with a bright smile. "Welcome to GWE! We'll get you settled in no time."

Ronnie gave a curt nod. "Sunny will handle everything. I have an urgent meeting." With that, he was gone.

Sunny chuckled. "Don't mind him. Come on, let's see if we can get you organised."

Over the next few days, she and the study assistants managed to get McKenna set up with all his basic needs, including an apartment.

There weren't many teachers around during the daytime on weekdays, but he did meet one colleague early on. Freddy was an extremely well-fed American. He waddled rather than walked.

"So, you're the new guy!" Freddy clapped him on the back. "Let me show you around."

As they walked through the glass-walled classrooms, Freddy pointed out supplies and lesson materials. "This," he tapped a stack of papers, "is my collection of lesson plans. Photocopy whatever you need."

Over lunch at McDonald's, Freddy asked, "So, you ever been to the Philippines?"

McKenna shook his head.

"Ah, you're missing out. Got a bar there, run by my girlfriend."

"What brought you there?"

"I served there in the US Army."

Freddy talked a lot about his girlfriend. There were honourable mentions for his ex-wives and ladies in general. He then announced he had to go. He was off to a gaming arcade to play the claw machine.

McKenna watched him toddle away. No end to this man's talents.

Alex was another colleague he met early on. Although small in stature, he was a larger-than-life character.

"How long have you been in China, Alex?"

"Just two years. Since I got married."

"Is your wife Chinese?"

"Yes. I met her in a KFC. I was here on holiday."

McKenna thought it a strange place to meet one's wife, but he was beginning to realise that this was China. Things like this happened as a matter of course.

McKenna soon saw that Alex was a little eccentric, whimsical at times, and prone to exaggeration. Despite being of Chinese extraction and having been in China for some time, Alex was still suffering from culture shock. He was very doubtful about Chinese hygiene.

He held up a tissue before approaching the bathroom door. "See this? Never touch with your bare hand. These cleaners use the same rag for cleaning toilets and door handles."

McKenna smirked. "You're not serious?"

Alex scoffed. "Believe me, Joe. You'll see."

Following training, McKenna and Alex were both assigned to the same Centre. The first week or two were tough. There were different types of classes and different levels of students. Sometimes the class had a lot of students, sometimes it was one-to-one.

One evening, after taking a class on football, McKenna sighed.

"Not a single one of them spoke."

"Why? What happened?" asked Alex.

"They were all girls. Not the slightest interest in football!"

Alex smirked. "Should've done a class on makeup."

"And what would I know about makeup?"

As time wore on, McKenna settled in and got to know the other teachers. They despised Ronnie and had nicknamed him Captain Mainwaring after the pompous Dad's Army character. One afternoon, McKenna went with Big Phil to the nearby Olde English Tea Rooms. Phil was a veteran of GWE and summed it up.

"It's a circus. Mainwaring is a bumbling fool. Strutting around the place, peering into classrooms like we're zoo animals."

McKenna shuddered as he sipped his tea. "Those bloody glass walls!"

Phil snorted. "They're there for a reason. Spying is the company's favourite pastime."

"Feels like we are in a goldfish bowl sometimes!" complained McKenna.

The Muslim restaurant downstairs was popular with the teachers because all dishes were cheap. Noodles were the staple food, but the teachers' favourite was their "fried egg sandwich." Sometimes, late at night, GWE staff called at a sushi bar in the metro station. The girls there would get giddy at the sight of Alex, winking at him and teasing him. They thought McKenna was the Centre manager and that Freddy was a pervert.

The students were a mixed bunch, aged between twenty and forty. They all took Western names for administrative purposes. Teachers often joked about who actually bestowed these names on them. Some of the most common were Coco, Minny, Winny, Maisie, Mandy, Sissy, and Gertie. Along with these was a fellow called

Handsome. In another class, he had the boy Winky and the girl Pinky. Winky was a stand-out character with his camp get-up. He was also a very good singer and was called upon at all parties.

In one class they liked to talk about Irish music. Most of them knew the Cranberries, Westlife, and U2, but few had heard of Van the Man or the Corrs. McKenna often engaged with Annie, a very talkative girl from Mongolia.

"Can you sing, Annie?"

"Ride a horse bareback no problem. But sing? No!"

Another student, Alfred, continually commented on McKenna being left-handed.

"How do you use chopsticks?" he blurted.

McKenna paused. "Just like everyone else!"

Alfred shook his head. "But you're left-handed!"

McKenna hadn't thought of left-handedness affecting that ability.

This group of students often invited McKenna to a nearby restaurant. They practised their English over dinner. Among them was a doctor by the name of Johnson. On one occasion, McKenna was suffering from a virus. Johnson noticed his discomfort. The following evening he presented McKenna with a bag filled with pills, drinks, sprays, rubs, and vapours. He refused to take any payment.

There was no shortage of odd characters among the students. Big Ben was known as the Shadow. He seemed to spend every waking hour in the Centre. He would go up to teachers and stand beside them. This could last for ages. Just standing there, saying nothing. While Ben was passive, Ernest was an active menace. Out of the blue, he would pop up at random locations. He would corner teachers and bombard them with questions. He was even known to follow teachers out onto the street.

At the end of May, Phil was transferred to another Centre. Mainwaring organised a going-away party at a Vietnamese restaurant for him and another departing teacher. Neither of the two turned up. They had probably had enough of Mainwaring. It didn't dampen the enthusiasm of the rest of the team. They celebrated for the absentees. Mainwaring was paying.

Alex knew how to wind everyone up. He constantly teased the Chinese staff about their love lives. He was big into sexual innuendo and talked a lot about the "Donkey Punch." Sunny had some idea what he was on about. The younger girls didn't but were still intrigued. Likewise, his classes often created a great sense of excitement among the students. One night he did an English Corner on Mickey Mouse which caused a huge commotion. A study assistant donned a Mickey suit. Spot prizes and snacks were handed out.

In June, Freddy travelled to the Philippines on one of his regular visits. When he returned, he dumped a bag of chocolates on the staffroom table.

"Help yourselves, folks."

"How was your trip?" everyone asked in unison.

"Angeles City was wild."

"Where did you stay?"

"With my girlfriend. But I had time to see a few other friends as well!" he boasted.

Tina, a study assistant, teased. "So, did your girlfriend know about your… other friends?"

Freddy winked. "I go out when she is asleep. After our sessions, she always sleeps like a log. But I never kiss anyone else, just her!"

"Romance isn't dead, folks," said Alex sarcastically.

They all laughed at the tale of the beautiful girl who had approached Freddy in a bar.

"It was only when I applied the speaking test that I saw her Adam's apple."

Alex was organising a night out soon after Freddy returned, but details were scarce.

"When is the party, Alex? Where will you have it?" ventured McKenna.

"How would I know?" snapped Alex. "I'm not the one who's organising it."

"But you were talking about it yesterday," replied a bemused McKenna.

Alex had turned very bitchy. It was the first time McKenna had seen this side of his character.

"You need to ask Sunny. She is in charge!" Alex asserted.

Conveniently for Alex, Sunny wasn't there to contradict him.

He went on. "You're always hogging the computer, McKenna," as he wandered around the teachers' room giving a running commentary on what he himself was doing. McKenna bit his lip. He decided it would be better to stay silent. He made sure to keep his distance for a few days.

It was early July before the night out at Party Pier came to pass. Despite the earlier denials, it was indeed Alex who organised it. Everything was booked in advance. When they arrived, they were escorted to a private room and seated on soft couches at a round table. Freddy was greatly taken by the scantily clad Russian dancing girl outside the club. It made his night when she posed with him for a selfie. He talked about it for days afterwards.

Next day, everyone at work wanted to see the photos, especially Freddy and the dancing girl. But Alex refused to upload them.

"Too busy," he said dismissively, not glancing up from his screen.

McKenna was fuming. "Playing power games again, Alex?"

It took days before Alex finally relented.

At GWE, any excuse called for a party. Staff were always on the move. Those that were popular always got a big send-off. So it was with Study Assistant Tina, who was leaving after several years of service. The venue was the Paddy Field Irish bar. McKenna lived near the bar and was there early. Bobby, a popular new teacher, arrived with a number of students. Everyone else came in dribs and drabs. Some got lost and had to be rerouted.

Bobby drank all night. Big Ben, the student, never left his side. Ben was smoking like a train and he too was drinking like a fish. Bobby was perched on a barstool, rabbiting on at 100 mph but totally incoherently. Ben was standing there in silence with his mouth wide open. He was completely enthralled and hanging onto every word of Bobby's whilst continuously exhaling huge clouds of smoke. Bobby was but partially visible. The only sure evidence of his presence was the voice coming from the pall of smoke.

Bobby wasn't long in the Centre before he began to make waves. Whispers of broken-hearted students, promises of love, abrupt abandonments. Students complained to teachers who complained to management. Mainwaring just shrugged it off.

"We'll restrict his classes to the mature ladies," he said, as if that solved everything.

Alex wasn't fazed either. "Bobby's no worse than half the people here," he remarked. "What about that manager caught shagging a student in the loo? Some kid filmed it. He confiscated her phone and it was never seen again."

Bobby and Alex both played soccer, but for different teams. Bobby bragged endlessly about his skills; Alex insisted Bobby was "only a sub" on his team. McKenna paid little heed. Rugby was his game. Later,

Bobby successfully ran a soccer tournament that Alex was supposed to organise.

"Nothing unusual there," thought McKenna.

Freddy was in high spirits most of September, fresh from another Philippines trip. He swanned in, decked in a new floral shirt, doling out the usual goodies to the staff.

"The wedding's back on!" he announced cheerfully. "She's in a better mood now."

Colleagues blinked. They had never heard a wedding mentioned before. Off or on!

All the rumours about Bobby were now out in the open and being discussed in online groups. One Monday morning, it came to a head. All the top brass gathered for a meeting. Afterwards, Mainwaring warned teachers not to discuss the matter any further.

"If I hear of anyone mentioning this subject again, online or offline, they will be fired!"

Alex missed the drama; he'd gone to visit his in-laws in Hubei. When he returned, he was in an odd humour. One afternoon, he was in the office with McKenna and Sunny when his wife called. Mid-conversation, he suddenly asked to speak to Mollie.

"Hi Mollie, how's your day going?" he cooed.

Sunny stifled a giggle. "Mollie's his cat," she whispered.

McKenna snorted. Alex looked up.

"Got a problem, McKenna?" he sneered. "Or are those cauliflower ears affecting your hearing?"

That did it for McKenna. Alex had crossed the Rubicon.

In fact, for McKenna the whole situation around the Centre was becoming a little sour. Mainwaring had just denied McKenna a full-time contract. Maybe it was time to move on. He went to see Big Phil at his new Centre a few days later.

"You're better off out of that snake pit," Phil agreed.

Phil's manager, Rex, happened to wander over. McKenna kept it casual. "Any chance of a transfer?"

Two days later, his phone lit up. It was Rex.

"Spoke to the CEO. Your transfer request has been granted. Start next month."

When Mainwaring heard the news, he wasn't best pleased.

"I went on holidays and when I came back you had decided to leave."

"Sorry, Ronnie. I just feel I need a change of scene."

"Could I ask you to reconsider? I'll give you more hours. I thought you were happy here."

"I've made my mind up," said McKenna with finality.

He was glad to be getting out.

On McKenna's last night, they had a party after work. Alex was in rare form, teasing the Study Assistants.

"Ever heard of the Hungarian Handshake?" he leered.

Sunny, loving the innuendo, giggled. "Stop! You're terrible!"

Freddy, meanwhile, was bragging about his most recent dalliance. "Left a young girl with a very big smile on her face."

McKenna sat sipping his drink, enjoying the chaos.

Out of the blue, Alex suddenly announced, "I'm afraid to have a baby."

McKenna was about to comment, but didn't. He did allow himself a wry smile.

"Kind of sums him up," he thought to himself.

Long Runs the Fox

When Joe McKenna arrived in China, his first point of contact was Ronnie Flanagan. Ronnie, a tall American with a whiskey nose, was the manager of the English Centre where McKenna was to teach. Great Wall English (GWE) had a network of training centres all across China. Ronnie was very helpful to McKenna, who was all at sea initially. He organised for him to get a bank account, a phone, and even an apartment. Then he showed him around the area.

Ronnie talked about his Irish heritage. He wanted to know all about McKenna, his culture and habits.

"Have you any observances?" he enquired. McKenna wasn't sure what he meant for a minute, but then it clicked. "No, not really."

"My grandfather was from County Clare," Ronnie declared proudly.

"Have you been to Ireland?" McKenna asked.

"No, not yet. I intend to go though. I would like to hook up with my cousins, if I can find them."

McKenna completed his training, his medical and all other preliminaries before settling into work. As he became familiar with life at the Centre, he began to see that it wasn't all sweetness and light between Ronnie and the other staff. He clashed continually with James Baker, a studious Liverpudlian. James was a conscientious professional and he detested Ronnie's disorganisation. In fact, few of the teachers had much respect for Ronnie. They saw him as an alcoholic, an arrogant man who rubbed people up the wrong way.

Ronnie was like all other managers, according to James – a lecherous creep. He always managed to schedule himself to teach the one-to-one classes with beautiful girls. He often had classes with Solace, a petite little lady with very striking features. He was very fond of her, although she was extremely wary of him. In time, McKenna got to know her too, as she confided in him. She had a difficult relationship with her mother, who had picked a man for her to marry. Girls in China usually followed their mother's wishes, but Solace refused point-blank.

After McKenna had been at GWE for a few months, a scandal erupted in Centre 3. A young American had joined the staff. Typical American, full of himself and handsome to go with it. He was breaking female students' hearts. One day it came up in conversation.

"Ronnie, are you aware that there's a little teacher wreaking havoc among the female students?" asked James.

"How do you mean?" replied Ronnie in an offhand kind of way.

"Pledging eternal love, having his way with them and then ignoring them."

Ronnie didn't seem particularly bothered.

"Ok. In future I'll try to allocate him classes with the more mature ladies, and men."

However, the problem didn't go away. Teachers kept getting complaints from students. Rumours continued to circulate. This eventually filtered through to Ronnie.

"I don't want to hear this issue being raised again. Any teacher found discussing it from here on in will be sacked."

The teachers were disgusted but felt powerless. None more than McKenna. He wondered if the welfare of the students mattered at all. Was it only the reputation of GWE that counted?

At the beginning, McKenna was on a part-time contract. He wanted to be made full-time. Ronnie kept procrastinating. McKenna eventually ran out of patience and decided to ask for a transfer. Soon afterwards, he was sent to Centre 2 on a full-time contract. Ronnie wasn't best pleased, but there was little he could do. McKenna wasn't long in Centre 2 before there was a big shake-up across GWE. Ronnie was demoted, but the reason never became known. He was reduced in rank and designated as a rover – a teacher who travelled around different centres as the need arose.

One day Ronnie was sent to Centre 2. McKenna was there.

"Hi Ronnie! How are you these days? Do you ever hear from any of our former students in Centre 3?"

"Not really. How about you?"

"I met Solace the other day," replied McKenna.

Ronnie's ears pricked up. "I didn't know you were in contact with her." He reddened.

"We just met for a quick coffee."

"I admire that girl," Ronnie asserted, without saying why.

Solace later told McKenna that Ronnie had contacted her that evening.

Two weeks later, McKenna again ran into Ronnie at Centre 2. That evening, Ronnie rang Solace. This time he was very direct.

"How would you like to meet in a hotel? I can book a room."

This was shortly before he was due to get married. Solace was very upset about the fact that he was about to tie the knot and here he was wanting to bring her to a hotel.

"Will you be inviting me to the wedding then?" she asked, cynically.

That really annoyed him and he hung up.

The next time Ronnie was sent to Centre 2, the same thing happened. He saw McKenna there and that evening he rang Solace. Again, she told him to get lost. She rang McKenna later to tell him. McKenna was wondering at that point if seeing or hearing from himself was a trigger for Ronnie to contact the girl. She was very annoyed and was now thinking about reporting him. McKenna knew she was a strong-minded girl. Perhaps Ronnie wasn't aware of that.

McKenna often went walking, and one day he happened to pass a newly opened restaurant. There were several girls outside distributing leaflets to passers-by. These were offering discounts to attract customers. McKenna stopped briefly. Next thing, he was being escorted in. Before long he was enjoying lunch – bitter melon stuffed with pork. When he had eaten, he went to the till. He was shocked to hear the lady there greet him with the words "Joe McKenna!"

He didn't recognise this woman at all, but she knew him.

"It's Lisa," she smiled.

He was waiting for the typical Chinese female's retort: "You don't remember me." He was mentally backpedalling at a furious rate. Maybe a student from GWE? Which Centre?

Then she put him out of his misery. "I'm Ronnie's wife."

Next thing, she took out her phone and made a call. She handed the phone to McKenna.

"Hi Joe. This is Ronnie Flanagan."

"Hi Ronnie. This is a surprise. What a coincidence!"

"Yeah. How was the lunch? Any comment on the menu? We're just open two days and learning as we go."

McKenna was no culinary expert, but he did make a few suggestions. "Perhaps you could add an English menu. And you ought to have cheesecake on it. Chinese ladies love cheesecake. Might I also suggest doing special promotions for groups of our students."

"Thanks Joe. We'll take all that on board. I like the idea of having students come."

McKenna went to pay but Lisa waved him away. "It's on the house."

Then she escorted him to the door. He was flabbergasted that this could happen – and he was just out for a stroll.

A few days later, McKenna decided to ring Ronnie to organise a night out at the new restaurant. He wanted to know if he could bring a group of students and whether the restaurant would offer a group discount. Ronnie didn't pick up on either occasion. McKenna wondered why, as the phone was ringing out.

Later that day, McKenna had a call from Solace to tell him she was being harassed by Ronnie. She was really angry and had now made up her mind to report him to his manager. McKenna too was very annoyed. Ronnie had managed to weave him into the story.

McKenna suspected there was a connection between him being in contact with Ronnie and Ronnie contacting Solace soon afterwards. It seemed to happen every time. She had received two calls from Ronnie that day. The first time, he had started off all loving and tender.

"I need you babes."

"I want you babe."

She had pleaded with him. "Please stop this, Ronnie."

Then in the second call, he turned nasty.

"Who was talking about me in Centre 3?"

"Who was responsible for getting me fired from my position as manager?"

"I think you know."

"How would I know?" she cried.

He became threatening. "All along, you've been talking to McKenna about me. Now I have the proof. McKenna rang me today, immediately after I contacted you. I could have you fired from your job. I'll go to see your manager."

When McKenna checked with Solace, it emerged that his unanswered call had been made just before Ronnie's second call to Solace. Ronnie thought McKenna had called him in relation to Solace. Coincidence and paranoia gone mad!!!!

On Ronnie's day off, Solace went into Centre 4 to see his manager. McKenna had asked her to leave him out of it. When she arrived, the manager wasn't there. She was resolute and called him the next day to arrange a meeting.

McKenna had earlier been granted permission for the student outing to the restaurant. Now he had to tell Peter, his manager, that it would have to be cancelled.

"I don't think we will be able to go through with the night out to Ronnie's restaurant."

"Why not?" asked Peter.

"I understand Ronnie may be in some trouble – better not to have any dealings with him just now."

Next day, McKenna was summoned to Peter's office.

"I've had a call from Ronnie's manager. There's been a complaint about Ronnie from a student. Can you tell me anything about what's going on?" asked Peter.

"I'd rather keep out of it."

"Okay. I understand. I don't blame you."

The following day, Peter questioned McKenna again.

"Can you tell me anything more about this business with Ronnie? I'm worried that a battery of TV cameras might arrive on the scene. Can you at least tell me if this is a major or minor scandal?"

"I don't think it's that great a scandal – unless there are more people involved that I know nothing about."

McKenna called Solace. She had met with Ronnie's manager.

"Hi Solace. How did it go?"

"I'm not sure. That manager is a slippery customer. I'm not sure I can trust him."

"They're all the same. GWE comes first."

"Well, if this complaint isn't taken seriously, I will go public. I will tell students and teachers all that has happened. The messages are still on my phone."

McKenna didn't hear any more for a while. He eventually rang Solace to check if there had been any developments. She had heard nothing more. McKenna then rang Peter.

"I was talking to that student who complained about Ronnie. She hasn't heard anything from GWE."

Peter feigned surprise. "That's strange. She should have had feedback. I'll mention it to Ronnie's manager. As far as I know, he has been disciplined."

That was it. There wasn't another word about Solace's complaint. It went nowhere – just another hushed-up case in a company more concerned with appearances than accountability. Frustrated but undeterred, Solace did what she had promised. She spread the word about Ronnie among the other female students.

Meanwhile, Ronnie's paranoia spiralled. Convinced McKenna was orchestrating his downfall, he began to behave oddly – showing up unannounced at Centre 2, questioning McKenna's students about him.

"Why is he so obsessed with you, Joe?" Solace asked McKenna after hearing about one of these encounters.

McKenna shrugged, uneasy. "Guilt? Or maybe he's just unravelling."

Things then took an unexpected turn. What with all the gossip, Ronnie's wife somehow got wind of what had been going on. She contacted Solace and arranged a meeting. Solace told her about the phone messages and also informed her that several other students had received similar messages. Lisa later managed to gain access to Ronnie's phone and was able to confirm the incriminating messages existed.

Enraged and humiliated, Lisa did what GWE wouldn't. She posted the incriminating texts online – tagging the school, their mutual contacts, even Ronnie's family. The fallout was instant. Parents demanded answers. Colleagues distanced themselves. Within days, GWE, fearing a scandal, fired Ronnie "for inappropriate conduct." Lisa threw him out of their apartment, he lost his share in the restaurant, and divorce proceedings were initiated.

McKenna and Solace met at a café months later.

"Well, Ronnie is well gone now. I heard he fled to Shenzhen," said McKenna, in a reflective mood.

"Funny," Solace mused, swirling her coffee. "GWE thought it would all just go away if they ignored me. But eventually Ronnie's own lies did for him."

McKenna nodded, watching the rain outside. "Long runs the fox."

"And GWE didn't fare too well out of it either!" she added.

"Indeed. Their reputation has been ruined. Student numbers have plummeted. I hear they are about to go bankrupt."

Mícheál O'Muis?

Charlie Bell was far from the average run-of-the-mill English teacher. A non-conformist, unconventional in his ways. Yet all those who knew him generally accepted his many eccentricities. Joe McKenna had worked alongside him and had known him for some time before he became aware of Charlie's Mickey Mouse fixation.

McKenna and Charlie were both teaching at Great Wall English (GWE). After work, they often socialised with various colleagues at "The Office," a small corner shop that sold beer. The woman who ran it had a few plastic stools and tables outside on the pavement. Random clients would appear, have a few beers and move on. It was here that McKenna first became aware of Charlie's infatuation with the American rodent.

Several teachers were sitting, chatting and watching the world go by. McKenna, Charlie, Denis and Brixton Bill were all there. After a few drinks, spirits were high. Out of the blue, Charlie launched into a tirade about Mickey. However, just as he was getting into his stride, a legless beggar came by. Charlie always attracted beggars. They knew him, and they knew he would always contribute to their pension fund. This fellow was travelling on a homemade trolley. Charlie's flow was interrupted as the man started pulling at his trouser leg. This was nothing new. It was the beggar's modus operandi.

While Charlie dealt with the beggar, Denis pleaded with his colleagues. "Don't let him get started on Mickey Mouse."

McKenna's curiosity was piqued. "Why not?" he asked.

Denis glowered. "Once he starts, he won't stop. It has got even worse since his visit to Disney Shanghai."

Despite the dire warning, McKenna wanted to hear more.

While Charlie was dealing with the beggar, the conversation moved on. Mickey was temporarily forgotten. That was until a few evenings later. As on the previous occasion, a number of GWE staff had gathered at The Office for after-work drinks. They had all had several beers. Naturally, there was a great sense of merriment. The regulars were joined by a relief teacher, Mr Maidstone, a tall, cultured American. His main claim to fame was that he accepted drinks from everyone but never bought any.

The free drink seemed to loosen Maidstone's tongue. He was rambling on about some obscure topic of no interest to those present. McKenna thought it would be a good time to change the subject.

"What's the story on this movie you're planning to make, Charlie?" Straight away, Charlie jumped to attention. His glasses nearly fell off and his face reddened as he launched into a rant about Mickey. "Mickey has become the biggest thing in China. I'm determined to do something about it!"

Maidstone sat there spellbound.

Denis wasn't best pleased. "You're stirring it, Joe."

Like Maidstone, McKenna too was taken aback at the depth and passion of this love-hate relationship with Mickey Mouse. Charlie continued, "I'm determined to drag Mickey through the gutter and destroy his reputation in the process."

He went on to describe how he was going to achieve this dubious or admirable objective, depending on how one looked at it. Most of the group listened intently as Charlie spoke of his upcoming movie about Mickey. Scenes would be shot in places like the Paddy Field bar, at the top of the Guangzhou Tower, along the Pearl River, in the Metro and in parks. Other possible settings were McDonald's, KFC, Pizza Hut, karaoke bars and nightclubs. Those who hadn't heard Charlie decry Mickey before were in stitches. Denis and Bill had heard it all many times. Heads down, they sat stoically through it all.

After a while, the revellers moved to the Paddy Field Irish Bar. The group came into contact with two Fijian pilots who were accompanied by a very pretty air hostess from Bolivia. Charlie was now fairly under the weather. He was hopping from one foot to the other and began to rant about Mickey, almost foaming at the mouth. It wasn't long before the trio sensed that all was not well. They quickly moved to another part of the bar.

Two English ladies then engaged Charlie in conversation. He recited some of his poetry for them and they were very impressed. However, he then started raving about Mickey. One of them made an innocent comment, Charlie passed a remark about the size of her bust and they too made good their escape. His colleagues drifted off as they saw Charlie deteriorate. Eventually, Denis had to bundle him into a taxi and bring him home.

Around this time, McKenna's friend Agnes arrived from Ireland. The two of them spent a week in Yangshuo and Guilin. When they returned to Guangzhou, they met up with Charlie. After having lunch, the trio went shopping. Agnes bought silk scarves, a jumper and a dress. McKenna bought a couple of belts. Charlie, as usual, was mesmerised by electronic equipment, gadgets and toys. He was looking at all sorts of gizmos and was about to buy a machine for sealing plastic bags. McKenna had to intervene and steer him in another direction.

They walked past a poultry shop where a tray of hens' feet was on display.

Pointing at them, McKenna enquired of Charlie, "Have you ever tried these?"

"I have."

Agnes chirped in, "I've had them a couple of times. An acquired taste, I must say."

She then addressed Charlie directly. "While we were in Guilin, we had a frog dish for dinner one evening."

"How did you find it?" asked Charlie.

"It was fine, apart from the number of bones."

"Would you eat frog, Charlie?" teased McKenna.

"I suppose I would if I was getting it for nothing," was the caustic reply.

Given Charlie's interest in Mickey, McKenna thought he would be interested to hear about the giant mouse they had seen in Guilin. He described it as being about the size of a rabbit. Agnes nodded in agreement. Charlie was having none of it. Impossible, he said. McKenna brought out his phone and showed him a photo of the animal. Charlie was totally nonplussed. He just wasn't able to take it on board.

They went on to Haizhu Square, a shopper's paradise. Souvenirs found in tourist shops elsewhere were available at wholesale prices. Charlie was greatly taken by a pair of red slippers on display in a shop window. He went inside and bought them on the spot. While he was inside the shop, he looked around and spotted a Mickey Mouse costume. He decided he had to have it too and the bargaining began. Eventually, the deal was done and he came away carrying Mickey in a black bin bag. He was delighted with his purchase.

They were shopped out at this stage and decided to retire to McDonald's. After eating his burger and fries, Charlie was still in a state of excitement. He decided to try on the Mickey costume. The Chinese customers and staff paid little heed to Charlie, although a few little kids were giggling and pointing. Perhaps it looked like an advertising gimmick. Even when Charlie ran around the restaurant jumping and shouting, no one batted an eyelid. Agnes and McKenna sat there bemused.

Charlie put the Mickey outfit away and then, without warning, launched into his Mickey tirade. Agnes never batted an eyelid. She took it all in her stride. Charlie went through his spiel about the upcoming movie featuring Mickey in various compromising positions. He ranted for about half an hour but eventually ran out of steam. They left and went their various ways.

McKenna wasn't long home when he got a call from Charlie.

"Are you wearing the Mickey Mouse suit?" McKenna enquired.

"No, Joe. Not at the minute."

"Are you not going to try it on?"

"I already did, just after I came in. It fits perfectly."

He went on, "I've just put on my new red slippers. They are so comfortable. It's like walking on air."

Charlie had recently moved to a new apartment in the outer suburbs. A few days later, McKenna was invited to visit. On arrival, Charlie showed him around the apartment and garden. McKenna spotted the black bag and assumed Mickey was still inside.

"When will your movie begin shooting?" McKenna asked.

Charlie was in practical mood now. "I need to buy a video camera first."

"Have you worked out the plot yet?"

"No. I'll just make it up as I go along."

"You must have some idea."

"Of course. I have a general outline in my head. It will feature the real Mickey and various imposters."

"Who is the real Mickey?"

"The original Mickey Mouse was created by Disney and Ub Iwerks in 1928 and initially named Mortimer. It is still the most recognisable image in the world, even beating Santa Claus."

Charlie then went on to discuss the imposters and some of their attributes. Chief among these, of course, was the Irish Mickey, the shillelagh-wielding Mícheál O'Muis. The Australian Mickey, coming from down under, would emerge from the depths of the Guangzhou Metro. He would mistake the Irish Mickey's shillelagh for a boomerang and end up totally disoriented.

The kilted, haggis-eating Scottish Mick McMuis would talk a lot but would be totally incoherent. Charlie wondered if he could find a set of bagpipes. It would go down really well to have the Caledonian Mouse playing them in the foyer of the Garden Hotel. The Nigerian Mickey's mantra would be "Guinness is good for you." This would enrage Mícheál O'Muis, who would claim that the Nigerian brand wasn't real Guinness at all.

Great Wall English was having a fancy-dress party for the students the following weekend and Charlie was determined to give Mickey an outing. He asked McKenna if he would take the costume with him and store it in his apartment, which was near GWE. Charlie put it in a large holdall for transportation. Denis had warned McKenna that the suit was in need of an airing. When the bag was opened, it emitted a most awful pong. Mickey had to be hung outside on the clothes line overnight.

The refreshed Mickey went down well at the party and there were selfies taken with many students. Afterwards, a group of students and teachers went for coffee and Charlie was giving further details of the upcoming Mickey movie.

He explained that there would be drunken Mickey scenes including the Nigerian Mickey and the fake Guinness. There was also talk of Mícheál O'Muis beating the Japanese Mickey with his giant shillelagh. In the end, all the fake Mickeys would have to be confronted by the true Mickey. He hadn't decided yet whether this would be singly or all together.

After the students had gone home, a few teachers decided to round off the evening with a visit to the Cave Bar, a notorious late-night venue. On the way, Charlie stopped to give money to a beggar. He also bought an XXXL Mickey Mouse poster off a hawker on the street. The security men in the Cave Bar saw the poster and confiscated it. But for some reason they allowed Charlie to bring in the holdall with Mickey inside.

The Cave Bar had many scantily-clad dancers, some dancing on the bar, some on tables and others in a cage. There was also a fair share of hookers hanging around, as well as an array of international customers, mostly from the Middle East. McKenna always got a great kick from watching the punters watching the girls. Their eyes would be almost popping out.

Charlie somehow managed to get into the cage with a girl and spent some time dancing with her. When he re-emerged, several hookers surrounded him but he showed little interest. His mind was on other matters. One of Mickey's white paws had gone missing. Meanwhile, he had been reunited with his Mickey poster. He promptly gave it to one of the ladies.

Charlie got very drunk and Denis had great difficulty getting him into a taxi. Denis later described it as like getting a bull into a trailer. Then, when he did get him in, he fell asleep. On arrival at the apartment, he had to get Charlie out of the taxi, carry him in and put him to bed.

At this time, Charlie was only seen occasionally. However, one night he did join all the regulars at The Office. A teacher known far and wide as "Captain Mainwaring" had just been transferred to the Centre and there was an obligation to have a welcoming party. Mainwaring was in fact a defrocked manager and McKenna had worked under him the year before. He had committed some unknown misdemeanour and been relegated to the role of humble teacher.

Charlie was in great form and soon had Mainwaring at his mercy, explaining the philosophical reasons for his great obsession with Mícheál Mouse. Once more he talked about how he saw Mickey as the biggest thing in China. "The Mouse was to be seen everywhere and was impossible to ignore."

Once Mainwaring was cornered, he was subjected to a very long rant about Mickey. Charlie's emphasis was on discrediting Mickey. His mission was to have him captured digitally in every embarrassing, degrading position that he could think of.

While Charlie ranted and raved, there were many lewd suggestions from the assembled group. Bill suggested that Charlie make a blue movie featuring Mickey and Minnie. Denis thought the two mice could feature in a peep show.

Charlie wasn't greatly taken with these ideas. Yet every time he talked about the movie, he added something new. This time, he was intent on adding a Swiss Mickey. Out of the blue, he stood up and began to yodel. Passers-by stopped and stood open-mouthed. He was going really well. But he overdid it. Just as he was hitting the high notes, his voice deserted him. The colleagues present collapsed with laughter. The onlookers continued to stare.

Mainwaring swallowed it all, hook, line and sinker. He stayed a lot longer than he intended and drank a lot more than he was used to. He eventually left the bar befuddled, baffled and bewildered.

Around this time, Charlie had a setback. His landlord decided to evict him from his apartment and put him on a month's notice. Charlie was very attached to his "gaffe" and upset at this development. But there was another side to the story. Neighbours had been complaining about the loud music. And then there was the shouting and yelling when Charlie came home drunk. Crowds of strange people would arrive at all times of the day and night.

Charlie was determined not to take this lying down. He decided to repaint the whole apartment with wall murals of the anthropomorphic murine before he departed. He worked at it for several days. Later, he enlisted a group of friends to speed up the work. Not only did they paint the walls but also doors, furniture, mirrors and anything else that was paintable.

The painting was finished about a week before the departure date. Charlie wanted as many people as possible to see the art and also maybe exhibit some of their own. He decided to turn the place into an art gallery for the last few days of his tenure.

Soon news of the event spread through word of mouth and a WeChat group, "Flat Art," was set up. On the day it was to open, there was a flurry of activity. People wanted directions, some wanted assurances on the safety of exhibits and others enquired about parking.

The party lasted for three days. Many visitors came to the house and several artworks were sold. Pride of place went to a mannequin bearing the head of Mickey Mouse. The rest of the Mickey costume had been lost along the way. Not to mention the brand-new video camera, presumably stolen by a visitor.

On the final evening, a huge crowd gathered and a bonfire was lit on some waste ground behind the apartment. Charlie had invited people to bring anything that needed incinerating. Unfortunately, one over-enthusiastic reveller brought the Mickey mannequin out and threw it on the pyre.

Charlie didn't even notice.

Guangzhou Blues

O f all the ladies Joe McKenna met in Guangzhou, Alice was the one he fell for. Head over heels. Perhaps it was the timing that made it so special. They first crossed paths on Christmas night, a night with its own sense of magic. The stars seemed perfectly aligned. Was it destiny? The beginning of a fairytale romance?

McKenna had been teaching at Great Wall English (GWE) for nearly a year. Christmas Day in China was a working day. After classes were over that evening, he was approached by Nancy, one of the more outgoing students.

"Come with us, Teacher Joe," she said, grinning. "Just me, Bee and Alice, three lovely ladies!"

"Where are you going?"

"To a bar."

"Why not," McKenna said. "It is Christmas, after all."

"Yes, we thought you would like to celebrate."

When they arrived at the bar, the festive atmosphere was palpable. Many expats had gathered to celebrate. The Pogues' "Fairytale of New York" was playing in the background. Everyone was in high spirits. The ladies ordered cocktails and McKenna had a cold Tiger.

Nancy organised a group selfie. "Everybody smile!" she beamed.

After a few drinks, Nancy and Bee decided to call it a night.

"I'll have one more before I go," declared McKenna.

Alice hesitated, then turned to McKenna.

"I'll stay too, Joe," she said. "If that's okay with you?"

He blinked. "Of course."

In hindsight, he had no clue whether this came about by accident or by Alice's design. He sensed a spark between them, some kind of chemistry. She talked about her family, her shop and her desire to learn English. At the end of the evening, he expressed the hope that they would meet again. He hinted that his birthday was coming up in a few days.

"Have you anything planned?" she enquired.

"Not yet," he replied.

He walked home in a daze. He was smitten. This lady had a certain presence, poise and grace. A delicate, oval face with well-defined cheekbones and a soft jawline. Her long black hair framed her face in a way that added to her allure, eyes that hinted at an unspoken sadness. She exuded a quiet confidence and charm. He felt he had just met someone very special.

The very next evening during class, Alice casually announced, "We're coming to your place for your birthday. We'll cook!"

On the day, the five ladies arrived at his apartment: Alice, Shammy, Yanny, Bee and Sunny.

It was like a whirlwind hit the place. They scrubbed, rearranged the furniture and took over the kitchen.

"Don't worry, Teacher Joe," Bee said. "Just you sit there. Relax."

Three of them went shopping, returning with groceries, wine, beer, juice and a cake.

Alice took charge of the cooking, issuing instructions as necessary. She glanced at McKenna once or twice, smiling when she caught his attention.

"Head chef?" he asked.

"I'm just good at bossing people," she replied mischievously.

Shortly before they sat down to eat, McKenna's friends, Charlie and Denis, arrived. They had chicken, vegetables, prawns and corn, though there was a small hiccup when someone complained, "The chicken needs more time!" Everyone laughed and the chicken went back in the pot.

After dinner came the cake, which was really delicious.

When the food and drink had all been consumed, the ladies didn't linger. They cleaned up and left.

The men headed to a bar.

"Well, Joe," Cha grinned, "you seem to have an admirer!"

"Which one?" McKenna teased.

"You know well, Alice! She only had eyes for you."

"Yes, I like her," McKenna admitted. "She is a bit special."

From then on, McKenna and Alice met regularly. There were visits to coffee shops, restaurants, malls and spas. Sometimes they would go as part of a group. Other times just the two of them. When they wanted to be alone, they met at the Greenery restaurant near where Alice lived. The Greenery had a good atmosphere and they would stay there for hours at a time. Sometimes a lady played music on a Chinese instrument. Alice had a persistent problem with a sore throat which she couldn't shake off.

She often ordered a reddish-coloured herbal tea. "It's good for my throat," she'd say. "Too much talking. Too much stress."

One night she confided, "Next September my son will start school. If I send him to school in Guangzhou, I have to pay 100,000 RMB."

He gasped. "That's crazy."

"Because I'm from another province," she explained.

"And your ex-husband?"

"Useless. He and his mother contribute nothing. Just criticism."

She looked away but couldn't hide her tears.

"I'm sorry," he said, unsure what to say.

"I always cry after talking to that woman," she whispered.

He nodded. "That's not right."

But part of him wondered why she was unloading her personal and financial problems on him, a relative stranger.

Alice loved massages. One day she brought McKenna to a blind massage centre, tucked away in an alley. "They're the best," she claimed. "Because they can't see, they focus on their sense of feel."

He didn't mention it, but he was pretty sure his masseuse wasn't blind; she was texting during the massage. She was very strong and gave him a thorough going over, ending with a very severe pummelling.

Alice had a man do her massage but she wasn't happy with him.

"He wasn't very good and he made me feel angry. But I do feel better than before."

The next time they went for a massage, it was to an upmarket spa in Tianhe. McKenna's boss had provided him with two vouchers. Alice was late as usual. When they got there, they were brought into a reception room and given tea. There was an array of staff present, all uniformed: masseuses, receptionists, attendants and a manager.

Firstly, Alice was led away. Shortly after, McKenna was brought off in a different direction. He was taken into a big room with a massage table, a round bath off to the side and a shower room. The lady gave him instructions in Chinese, made some hand signals and left.

Alice then rang from wherever she was and told him what he had to do. This involved showering and changing before lying face down on the table. The masseuse then came back and gave him a really soothing massage.

Afterwards, he went to reception and waited for Alice. She had enjoyed her massage too but thought it was a relaxing massage rather than a health massage. They had more tea and were given more vouchers for the next visit.

A few weeks passed. Even though they continued to meet regularly, McKenna felt there was something amiss. They weren't getting any closer. There was no sign of a relationship developing. There was no intimacy. Zero.

Alice was giving him mixed messages and asking questions he couldn't answer without risking her ire. She would ask:

"Why do you like me?"

"What are you thinking about right now?"

"Do you think she's prettier than me?" (a nod toward a passing lady)

"What's wrong?" (when nothing seemed wrong)

And when he answered cautiously, she'd frown. "You're hiding something."

She would complain of feeling unwell but never say why. Her mood swung unpredictably. At times she seemed to find fault with everything. McKenna felt helpless, emotionally adrift from her.

Alice was cautious. She had had a very bad marriage and didn't want to repeat that experience. She worried that McKenna might just up and leave. She wanted to keep him at a distance while she got to know him better.

"You could leave China anytime."

"I have no plans to do that."

"You could just disappear back to Ireland!"

"Why would I? I have my work here."

She didn't speak it but she wasn't sure if he would be willing and able to take care of her. And most importantly, her son. She kept testing him. He kept failing.

As time moved on, the distance between them increased. No longer the cosy nights in the Greenery. They still met, but usually now as part of a group. When they were occasionally alone, there were always more questions, more doubts. No resolution. She had constant problems with her throat. Never happy.

One night, McKenna went with Alice and her friend Shammy to a very busy restaurant in Xiaobei. Customers were eating, drinking beer and rolling dice. She ordered a big pot of broth containing prawns, rice and frogs.

The broth was supposed to help Alice's throat. "Not as good as the last time," she said, pushing the bowl away.

When Shammy wandered off, Alice leaned over. "Should we be together?" she asked doubtfully.

"How can I answer that?" he replied.

Later that evening, she texted: *I don't think it's a good idea.*

He sat for some time just staring at his phone.

Alice's problems were insoluble. He felt he was now one of them. No matter what he did, it didn't please her.

Cha had meanwhile been to Thailand and had brought back a sarong for McKenna, who thought Alice would like it. It might cheer her up. He rang her but all he managed to do was wake up her sleeping son. The boy started to cry and the call had to be terminated.

Even though Alice wasn't happy with McKenna, she still texted him. Her emotions were all over the place. One minute she was for him, the next against him. Her birthday came and he bought her a necklace. She was all delighted with it for a while. After receiving it, Alice treated Shammy and McKenna to dinner in a restaurant near GWE. In the restaurant, Alice was picking at him. She scolded him after dinner.

"You've eaten too many dumplings."

"You're too fat."

"Your table manners need to improve!"

Then came an episode which was typical of how things were between them. Alice had gone off on her own to Shenzhen for a couple of days to "clear her head and think." On her way back, she texted to say she wanted McKenna to go to a spa with her that night and stay over.

When they arrived at the spa, Alice gave him some instructions, then she went one way and he another. The place was packed. They lost each other. No one spoke English.

Then she appeared again. "Are you OK? Are you able to sleep on a recliner?"

"I don't know. I'll try."

"I'm going to sleep. If you're not happy, you can go home."

"I'll have a walk around first."

Some time later he decided to look for a recliner. He couldn't find one that was vacant. There were hundreds of people in the place. The recliners were all taken. Nor could he see Alice.

Totally frustrated, he decided to go home. When she found out, she was furious.

"You should've told me!"

"How? I couldn't find you."

Even the next morning she was still upset. It was Valentine's Day. A far cry from Christmas.

A few days later she called him and wanted to talk. Then she told him she still couldn't make up her mind about him. Surprise surprise!

After all the toing and froing with Alice, McKenna increasingly began to question whether it was worthwhile. He suspected they were heading nowhere slowly, even if he didn't admit it fully. There was no joy in it any more. It was impossible to please her. Arguments without conclusions. Texts that went round and round. She seemed to be evaluating his worth, his future. They began drifting and met less and less. Just the occasional call.

She didn't want him, but she didn't want anyone else to have him either. When she saw him talking to other women, she grew jealous. Once, in a Starbucks with Alice and Sunny, Alice lingered far longer than she wanted to, just to avoid leaving him alone with Sunny.

She had noticeably changed her image. Short hair, new clothes, always dressed up. She was still prone to bouts of sickness, tiredness and depression. One day, McKenna met her in the centre. She gave him a bag of sweets. Then she started:

"Have you found a girlfriend yet?"

"You've put on weight!"

He also heard she had been telling her troubles to Mr Maidstone, another colleague.

In the summer, she finally made some big decisions. She quit her shop. Her family moved back to her hometown. She got a new apartment, a new job, and a cat.

"It has blue eyes like you," she informed McKenna during a rare meeting.

"Maybe we're related," he replied sarcastically.

One night they arranged to go to a small restaurant near McKenna's apartment. When he arrived, he saw Shammy's bike was parked outside. Inside, the tension was palpable. Alice barely spoke. The frosty atmosphere got to Shammy. "Dogs like bones!" she blurted out of the blue. They ate up and went their separate ways. There was nothing more said.

They never met again. No dramatic ending. They just drifted apart. Alice could be radiant, magnetic, but she was also erratic, moody, wounded. McKenna understood her pain, but couldn't bridge the gulf between them. Though still fond of her, he was weary of the constant ambiguity. Perhaps it just wasn't the right time.

Alice needed more than McKenna could give. He couldn't offer the stability, commitment, emotional depth or financial security she craved. She suspected he might be a flirt.

While McKenna never saw Alice again, he did keep in contact with a few mutual friends.

One evening, about a year later, he met Sunny for dinner.

"How are you these days, Sunny?"

"I've got a new job now. I'm working for Bank of America. How are you getting on?"

"It's fine. The students keep me busy. How are all our old friends?"

"I don't see many of them now. I finished my course and I don't go to GWE any more. Most of them moved on. I still see Yanny, that's about all."

"How about Alice?"

"Alice is in California. She married an American businessman a few months ago. Herself and her son have gone to live there."

He was visibly gobsmacked. Sunny never knew of his connection with Alice, but she saw his reaction.

"You know I was very close to Alice at one time?" he confessed.

"No Joe, I didn't."

"We used to meet every day."

"Well, I heard she met this guy and married him soon afterwards. I think she was always on the lookout for a rich westerner."

"I think you're right, Sunny. I didn't fit the bill."

Charlie Visits the Ancestral Temple

One time Charlie Bell took a notion that he would visit a temple in Foshan. Joe McKenna was cajoled into accompanying him on this adventure. The latter was a reluctant companion. Hadn't he already visited many Chinese temples? Did he need to see another one? He wasn't sure if the temple was Charlie's sole focus either. It was possibly a cover for some other nefarious activity.

Be that as it may, McKenna was up bright and early and ready to go. He was doing some jobs around the house when he got a text message. Charlie was waiting at Martyrs Park metro station. It was nearby. Ten minutes later they were on the metro to Xilang.

Charlie was in great form, discussing his various projects, plans and ideas. He moved seamlessly between all sorts of intentions, conceptions and happenings. He began by relating a story about a man back in Ireland who had brought up a fox from a cub and tried to mate it with a Pomeranian dog. McKenna never got to hear the outcome as it suddenly occurred to Charlie that McKenna might like to hear some poetry. Charlie loved reciting, mostly his own compositions.

"Would you like to hear a poem, Joey?"

"Why not? What else would I be doing anyway?"

"But first, ring me!" Charlie ordered.

So McKenna rang Charlie's number. Instead of the expected ringtone, he heard Charlie launching into a poem about Guangzhou. He described the city, sequentially using all the letters of the alphabet.

It wasn't the first time he had heard the poem. Charlie had recited it before on several occasions. He especially remembered a rendition on a night of mayhem in the Paddy Field Irish Bar. His listeners then had included two pilots and a flight attendant. After they had praised his artistic talent, Charlie had seen fit to insult all three. On this occasion the phone went dead halfway through the recitation. That was the end of that.

McKenna was keeping an eye on their whereabouts. At Xilang they had to change lines.

"Come on Charlie. Let's go. We have to change to the Foshan line."

Things now got complicated.

"Let's have a look at the map in the station before we get on," suggested McKenna. "We know our destination is the Ancestral Temple in Foshan?"

"Yes, that's the one," said Charlie confidently.

"I googled it before we set off. I have the name of the station written down in English."

"What is it?" asked Charlie.

"It's Tongji Lu station."

"I can't see it," said Charlie, wiping his glasses.

"No wonder," said McKenna. "The names on the map are all in Chinese and Pinyin. There's no English."

After some thought he suggested, "Let's try the third one from the end."

"Sounds good to me," replied Charlie.

When they got off the train, they examined the local map. Again, no English. Nor was there any indication that the temple was in the vicinity. They went up to ground level to have a look around anyway. There was nothing resembling a temple that they could see. They took a walk around the area but drew a blank. They then decided it must be the next stop.

So they went back into the metro and travelled to the next stop. This time they came up in a wilderness. There was nothing much there at all, just a field of weeds. After that, the next stop was the terminus. They decided they might as well try there. There was surely a good possibility that the temple was in the city centre.

When they reached the terminus they surfaced again and had a good walk around. There was nothing to suggest a temple there either. Charlie did spy an electronics shop. He was in there immediately. He wanted to buy some utterly useless gadget. It took McKenna about ten minutes to get him out.

It was now lunchtime. They decided to eat in a small place outside the metro station. They were charged 25 RMB despite everything on the menu being priced at 15 RMB. Some things just can't be explained. Yet another mystery of the Orient.

While they were having their chicken, rice and vegetables, they had a brainwave. Their colleague Denis might know the location of the temple.

"Let's ring Denis," suggested Charlie.

"Great idea! But isn't he in class at the moment?"

"Sure, we'll try him anyway."

"I suppose I'll call. Your battery's gone, isn't it?"

Luckily Denis answered.

"How's the trip going?"

"We can't find the temple."

"Where are you?"

"We're at the end of the line in Foshan."

"Okay, go four stops back."

Denis said the name in Chinese but it meant nothing to McKenna.

"I'll put Charlie on."

Both Charlie and Denis understood some Chinese. Denis gave the name of the station to Charlie in Chinese. Just for good measure, he also gave him the names of the stations before and after it.

They departed the restaurant and were making their way back to the subway when they came upon a Greek restaurant, right opposite the metro entrance. A few people were sitting outside drinking coffee. They couldn't resist having a closer look. Inside they could see two ladies tucking into moussakas.

They had paused only momentarily but it was long enough to alert the Greek owner who suddenly appeared at their side.

"Good morning gentlemen. Are you American?"

"No way," stated Charlie emphatically, "We're Irish."

"Nice to meet you. I'm Darius. Welcome to Foshan. I've never been to Ireland but I believe it's a beautiful country. Friendly people too."

"It's a pity we've already had lunch," said McKenna regretfully.

"Come in anyway. You must meet my wife, Fan."

A Chinese lady came towards them smiling.

Charlie held out his hand. "Nice to meet you, Fan."

McKenna bowed to her as he greeted her. "Good morning, Fan."

"Please sit down," urged Darius as he ushered them to a table.

Next thing, the menu was brought out.

"I'll have a coffee," said Charlie.

"Green tea for me," added McKenna.

Charlie spotted a lady eating Greek yoghurt. "I'll have one of those too, please."

"I make it myself," Darius proudly announced.

The yoghurt had honey on top and came with two spoons.

"Why don't you try it, Joe?" invited Charlie.

After a spoonful McKenna was hooked. "It's delicious. Can I order a bowl for myself?"

"Of course," replied Darius.

Meanwhile, the drinks came. Charlie liked the coffee. McKenna's tea tasted really good. Their host then brought out cakes. Darius sat down with them and showed them pictures of his five-year-old daughter. He said she was very cute. Who were they to disagree?

The two intrepid travellers ate and drank their fill before departing the café. Darius saw them to the door. There was still the unattended business of the temple. Into the metro they went once more. They did come out at the right station this time. However, they had to call Denis again to direct them from there.

McKenna had a touch of déjà vu as they approached the temple. They were walking along a street with a high grey stone wall on one side. Sure enough, he had been here before but couldn't remember when or with whom. Nevertheless, it didn't dampen his enthusiasm. They went into the temple and took some pictures, as one does at these kinds of places. It was as most temples are.

They came on a kind of amphitheatre. Somehow Charlie discovered there would soon be a show starting, the High Stakes Lion Dance (not to be mistaken for line dance). Apparently, it was a very famous ritual and was enacted three times a day.

In the meantime, they went for a walk around the complex. McKenna was admiring all sorts of Buddhas and mythical beasts. Charlie had nothing else but the Lion Dance on his mind. After about ten minutes he decided the show would be starting and rushed off. McKenna had got talking to three girls. They wanted to have their pictures taken with him and he stayed talking with them for a while. For the selfie, they posed by the side of a red elephant, not a real one!

McKenna moved on to the show to find Charlie sitting in the front row, mesmerised by the performance. There were a couple of lions cavorting about in the space before him. There were two men inside each lion. The lions were doing all manner of leaps, contortions and tricks.

Along the side of the performing area there were two parallel rows of posts or stakes, each about two metres high. The lions jumped up there and started leaping around from post to post. The two lads inside each lion had to be perfectly in sync. Their performance was a mix of dance and martial arts. They watched this for a while. Charlie was spellbound. After a bit there was a lull in the show and McKenna dragged Charlie away. He wanted to have a look around Foshan before they went home.

Near the temple was a kind of old town. It was packed with tourists, both Chinese and foreigners. They walked around window shopping. Luckily enough, there weren't many gadget or gizmo shops to take Charlie's fancy. They decided they needed a rest and adjourned to a coffee shop before making the return journey.

Just as McKenna thought they had navigated their way safely out of Foshan without any unnecessary purchases, Charlie spotted a gift shop. He was in there before his friend could stop him.

"Isn't that stool just lovely," drooled Charlie. Nothing would do but he would purchase it.

Just as he was on the way out he spotted something else. "Oh look at that blue porcelain pig, I have to have that."

It was a long pig and had a slot on its back for inserting coins. The shop owner obviously saw Charlie coming. "The pig comes as part of a set of two."

The other pig was a kind of pinky colour and had a rotund shape. Before long the pigs were wrapped and ready. Charlie paid in cash and they were on their way with the stool and the brace of ceramic swine in a plastic bag.

As they walked to the metro McKenna queried Charlie. "Why did you buy those pigs?"

McKenna thought there was absolutely no need for them. Charlie was miffed.

"Well, I wanted to bring back some kind of present for Denis. He always does a lot for me."

"But wouldn't he wonder why he was getting a pig?"

"I'm thinking about which one to give him!"

"Do you think he wants or needs a piggy bank?"

"He might like the pink one but I will give him a choice."

When they were seated on the metro Charlie took out the two pigs. He started to examine them, turning them over and over.

"I like both of them. I can't bear the thought of having to give one to Denis."

McKenna noticed something amiss. "The blue pig has a hole in its belly. It has no bung."

Charlie was dismissive. "That's no problem. It can be blocked with banknotes."

Whatever it was about the metro, it brought out Charlie's storytelling side. On the return journey the animal theme continued with another doggy tale. He once had a dog called Heaney which led quite a roving life. He said the dog often used to get lost. It fell out of his van once in Ballymote and was found 25 miles away in Drumshambo. He had to regularly pick him up from police stations in England when he was domiciled in that country.

Charlie also claimed the dog could talk but gave no examples. He said it got very upset when he smoked dope. Heaney had it figured that if Charlie was smoking weed he wouldn't get a walk that day. He would bark furiously every time Charlie lit a joint. Charlie also told of a time when the dog found his stash, took it out into the garden and hid it. However, Charlie failed to mention that he had it well trained for some rather dubious activities. According to Denis, Charlie had once sent it into a tent on Rathlin Island to relieve the owner of a bottle of poitín.

McKenna and Charlie met a few days later.

"Why the long face?" asked a puzzled Charlie.

"I was talking to Denis," said a downbeat McKenna.

"So was I," claimed a smiling Charlie. "How did you get on?"

"Actually, I was looking forward to telling him about the adventure in Foshan, the Lion Dance, the red elephant, the Greek restaurant and the surprise coming his way."

"What happened?" enquired Charlie.

"He wouldn't let me speak. In fact, he was downright rude. All he said was, 'Once you have seen one temple you have seen them all, once you have seen one Buddha you have seen them all.'"

"Same here," confirmed Charlie who was grinning from ear to ear. "He snubbed me too. He was very disdainful."

"Why do you look like you just won the Lottery?"

"When he took that attitude, I decided to withhold his pig. Now I have the two of them for myself," gushed Charlie as he rattled the two porkers around in his bag.

Catching a Tartar

Joe McKenna first met Susan on Bastille Day 2012 at the Friendship Store in Taojin. Like several of his great romantic misadventures, it began online. Everything had progressed smoothly and they had exchanged information on their likes, dislikes, hobbies, music, and favourite holiday destinations. Things had gone so well they decided to transition to the offline phase of relationship building.

The rain was bouncing off the pavement and Susan was late. Finally, she rushed up, shielded by an umbrella.

"Sorry I'm late," she said breathlessly. "Something cropped up at the last minute."

"It's okay. You're here now. What would you like to do?"

"I know a restaurant nearby. The Banana Leaf."

"Yes, I've heard of it. Never been."

"Okay. Let's go!"

The restaurant was medium-sized. Though busy, it had a cosy and intimate feel with its soft lighting and warm colours. The prospects for romance looked promising. For him, there was the bonus of an English menu. They ordered several dishes.

Despite having just met McKenna, Susan didn't dwell long on pleasantries. They were barely seated before she launched into a tirade about the world and its father.

"Why do people do so many stupid things, cause problems, and try to control others?"

When she realised he had no intention of replying, she backtracked.

"Maybe they just… care too much," she said, rolling her eyes.

He was caught off guard by this novel form of bonding. She did rest her case while she ate, but it wasn't long before she resumed. This time she focused on two specific people, one an ex-boyfriend and the other a platonic friend. Both were good to talk but poor listeners. She didn't indicate whether they were among those she was referring to earlier.

Seeing as she was drawing no response from him, Susan changed tack.

"Joe, you're not the only Irishman I know," she teased. "I have a friend from Dublin. He often visits Guangzhou."

"How do you know him?"

"From when I worked in import-export. I introduced him to a factory that makes O'Neills sportswear."

"O'Neills is a very popular brand in Ireland," McKenna declared.

"A potential business opportunity here," he thought.

Susan then received a phone call.

"Sorry, I have to run. Sister needs me to babysit."

She asked for a doggy bag and took away the leftover food. They agreed to keep in contact.

By the time they met again a few days later, McKenna had temporarily set aside the minutes of the first meeting.

"I'll bring you to a Szechuan restaurant," suggested Susan.

"Okay. You chose well the last time."

"It's a small upstairs place. The food is very spicy."

"Don't worry. I like it hot."

When they arrived it was very busy.

"Sorry, Joe. There is no English menu but I will order," Susan said apologetically. "Just remember it will be very spicy."

Time proved that she wasn't exaggerating. A big pot of soup was brought out and set on a heater in the centre of the table. The soup contained a large fish, vegetables, and noodles. They also had sticky rice and he ordered beer. It was really enjoyable but so hot McKenna went through a packet of tissues during the course of the meal. Susan again asked for a doggy bag.

Afterwards, they went to McDonald's for ice cream and in the course of their conversation Susan talked about a friend who had called her earlier. She was very concerned, even angry, about this man's situation and what had befallen him. McKenna now remembered their first encounter and guessed this was one of the men who had been spoken about at that time.

"I'm very worried about my friend Bruce."

Without further ado she commenced to narrate part of Bruce's biography.

"A few years ago he was living happily with a girlfriend in Brisbane. However, after twelve years they broke up. It hasn't gone well for him since."

She continued, "He left Australia and went to Thailand where he took up with a hooker and lived with her for six years. Then they moved to China but the lady didn't like it there. It wasn't long before she returned to Bangkok and resumed her former career."

Susan described the Thai lady in very unflattering terms. She got very worked up about how her Aussie friend had fallen for this lady.

"My friend has been used. His confidence and self-esteem are both at rock bottom."

She drew breath before resuming, "On one occasion, when I was in a restaurant with him, he tried to slit his wrists."

"That sounds bad!"

"It sure was. He was hospitalised and I was traumatised. But he didn't mean to do it. It was really a cry for help."

McKenna could see that she was visibly shaking.

He felt like a rabbit in the headlights. Mesmerised. Was Susan using him as a sounding board or a scratching post? It wasn't the first time in his life, nor would it be the last, that he had found himself hung out on the end of this kind of diatribe. There were so many people living in her head; ex-boyfriends, friends, a friend's ex-girlfriend, and an Irish businessman. Such were the perils of 21st-century dating.

Susan droned on but McKenna's thoughts were elsewhere as she wound herself up. At some point she read his thoughts and knew she would be better to change topic. She rounded off by stating that this was all about her philosophy of life. He wasn't sure if this philosophy included trying to connect to the person in front of her. He thought to himself, "Where is the romance here?"

The Australian man was unloading on Susan who was then unloading on McKenna. Was the logical progression for him to unload all this on the next random person he met?

Susan moved on to her life at university.

"When I first began to study at university my mother wouldn't pay my fees."

"Why not? Had she no money?"

"No, Joe. It was because I didn't study the course she had chosen for me."

"What did you do?"

"I thought I would have to drop out but, as luck would have it, I was rescued by an ex-employer. He stepped in and paid all my expenses."

As a result of this intervention, Susan maintained she had to help others, just as she had been helped herself. McKenna wondered if he was about to receive some unforeseen assistance and what form it might take. Unfortunately, he didn't have a chance to hear the details. He had to rush home to get ready for work.

"When will I see you again?" she asked.

McKenna hesitated. He wanted to back off a little. He knew he needed a break before meeting Susan again. So he kicked to touch.

"I'll get back to you in the next few days. I'm not sure of my work schedule yet."

He was attracted to her but her constant ranting was giving him a lot of food for thought. Was it a question of waiting until she had purged all the poison from her system? He did want to keep Susan sweet. He always had it in the back of his mind that she might be able to facilitate some business with the sportswear company.

It was over a week before they met again.

"Which restaurant would you like to go to this evening?" enquired McKenna.

She surprised him. "How about we go for a walk this time?"

As they walked along she decided to stop at a shop to buy some shirts for her brother.

"There is a special offer today. I'll buy three. Why don't you buy three too?"

"They're too dear." He wasn't in a shirt-buying mood that evening.

After leaving the shirt shop they went to McDonald's. While she worked her way through her McFlurry, she debated with herself the relative merits of marrying and not marrying.

"After I finished university, I worked hard and thought little about marrying."

"You were still very young," McKenna ventured.

She went on, "Then I took a less stressful job, hoping that would allow me more time to find a husband."

"And how did that go?"

"Look at me. Five years later. I'm still single."

She shrugged her shoulders as she went on.

"I've made up my mind. I'm going to have to forget all about men and go back into the stressful environment where I can earn more money."

McKenna felt that he may as well not have been there. He still couldn't figure out why she felt she had to tell him all this. He wondered about the purpose of their meetings. He kept reminding himself that he had met this lady on a dating site. Any time he broached the subject of romance he was immediately rebuked. She didn't want to talk about that at all. Where exactly did he fit into Susan's world?

She mentioned that her Aussie friend had gone back to his homeland. McKenna braced himself for a further instalment on the life of Bruce. Thankfully, this time there were other things on her mind, as she now turned to her job search. She had received one job offer but she didn't want to take it. There was also the possibility of a second interview at a company she did want to work for. So far she hadn't heard back from that one.

He was very tired and just about got through this session. She eventually went home and before parting she asked him to call her when he was free. Once again, for him, there had been no feeling of being on a date. There wasn't the slightest suggestion of romance anywhere on the horizon despite all the hours of talk and time spent together. He was no more than an onlooker as Susan carried on this constant debate with herself.

Susan went quiet for a few days. That was until one day, as he was out walking, he received a text from her asking to meet. She had just finished another interview in Zhujiang New Town and was heading his way. He agreed without thinking but then regretted his decision. When she arrived, initially she was all bright and breezy. They went to a Chinese restaurant across the highway from his apartment and had a very pleasant meal which included a bowl of fish heads, a new one for McKenna. To his surprise he found them delicious.

In his estimation, Susan was seldom not scolding about something. They had hardly finished eating before she started. On this occasion, it was about the man who had recently interviewed her and McKenna again had to play the role of silent witness. This man's crime was that he had offered her a paltry salary. She was swearing in English, which he found unusual. He thought Susan had ordered too much food and indeed there was quite a lot left over. As they were leaving, she again asked for a doggy bag. He kept wondering what she was doing with the food she was taking away.

McKenna's brother Mark then came to visit and Susan joined them one evening. They went to a big seafood restaurant by the Pearl River. He did note, though, that in Mark's presence, Susan's Australian friend wasn't mentioned once.

After Mark had left for the airport Susan wanted him to go off with her for the afternoon. He said he was too tired and asked her to wait for a couple of hours. So he went home, slept for a while, and met Susan later. He was surprised when Susan appeared wearing a T-shirt and a skirt with the O'Neills GAA insignia. Was it just to remind him of her connections in the sportswear company?

They decided to go to Beijing Lu as Susan wanted to buy a bag. She searched high and low but no bag pleased her. She did find a couple of clasps for her hair. She hadn't said as much but McKenna suspected she had a final interview coming up. Tired out after the shopping, they went for dinner in a Cantonese restaurant where Susan ordered pork, fish, vegetables, rice, and a portion of chicken feet. There was again a surplus of food and once more Susan requested a doggy bag. Was she taking the leftovers home to feed her family?

After dinner they walked all the way back to Taojin and it took an hour because Susan was walking slowly and stopping frequently for rests. McKenna suspected she had something bothering her and wanted to talk about it but didn't know how or where to begin. Probably more comfortable talking to herself, he thought.

She did talk generally about love, relationships, emergency love, and money. She complained about men who bought her one drink and wanted to go to bed with her. Then she specifically mentioned the Australian friend as well as a previously unknown American friend. There was also the Irish businessman, who spent a lot of money on holidays but had no wife. However, McKenna had a feeling she still hadn't touched on the issue that was bothering her. He guessed it was to do with the job applications.

Approaching Taojin a strange thing happened. They sat down on a low wall outside an international hotel. There were several hookers around and one was patrolling up and down past them, obviously on the lookout for an international customer. McKenna was sitting a little bit apart from Susan.

One hooker walked past a few times and spotted this separation.

"Is he your boyfriend?" enquired the hooker, gesturing towards McKenna.

"No he's not," replied Susan, shaking her head.

The hooker then asked Susan for permission to go off with him. Susan didn't reply to the lady but told McKenna in English what was going on. He had a feeling Susan was totally indifferent to whether he went off with the hooker or not. The tart paused briefly. When he showed no signs of movement, she spotted a more likely victim emerging from the hotel and made a beeline for him.

Susan texted the next evening, a Friday, and wanted to meet but McKenna made an excuse and said he had to teach a class. It was too soon. He arranged to meet her on Monday evening when he finished work. By this stage he had come to the conclusion that there was little possibility of a romance with Susan. But there was still the sportswear business to think of.

When Monday evening came it was raining heavily and Susan texted to ask him to go to a mall in Tianhe. She was already there and didn't want to go outside and get wet. So he set off in the rain. When he arrived they went to dinner at an upmarket Thai restaurant. There was a live pop group entertaining the diners.

While the customers ate, the band played. As part of their act the musicians kept moving around the restaurant. They would play a few tunes in one place and then move to the other end of the restaurant taking all their guitars, drums, and equipment with them. He wondered if this was common practice with Thai bands.

Despite this novel form of entertainment, it hardly lifted his spirits. Susan was again very argumentative. And once more she pulled her stunt of ordering too much food, getting a doggy bag, and taking the leftovers away. McKenna was boiling inside but kept his counsel mainly because he was still thinking of the possible business opportunity.

They left the restaurant and went for coffee downstairs but Susan was still very twisted. She castigated him because he had asked for an update on her job search. He didn't respond; there was no point in becoming embroiled in an unwinnable argument.

When they emerged from the building it was still raining very heavily.

"Let's get a taxi," said Susan.

McKenna went out on the road but there were so many people and so few taxis it was futile.

"We won't get a taxi for hours. There are dozens of people waiting out there."

"Be patient."

"It's impossible. The metro is only five minutes away."

"It's at least half an hour's walk! I'm not moving!"

He was sure there was a station nearby. After a brief stand-off he decided enough was enough. He had reached the end of his tether. He just walked off and left her there. Business or no business, he was heartily sick of Susan. In that instant he decided he would never see her again. Nor did he.

Now it was McKenna's turn to debate with himself, but without a witness. He asked himself why he had wasted so much time and effort. In the end there had been no romance, no business, and he had been used as an unwitting food bank. The whole affair had been nothing more than a damp squib which fittingly began in the rain and finally fizzled out in a downpour.

The Father Cat

I t was his day off. Felix Murray lay in bed, staring at the ceiling, listening to the rain tapping at the window. His flatmate Jimmy had gone to work, but Murray was not alone. Jimmy's brother had come to "visit" a few weeks earlier and now seemed to have moved in for good. He was like a shadow, always there. Murray was sick of the sight of him, permanently stationed at the computer. Before Murray even got up, he heard Jimmy return, and soon afterwards the two of them left together.

For Murray, the highlight of the day was his date with Linda. They had agreed to meet outside McDonald's at the nearby mall. He waited, scanning the crowd, until his phone buzzed.

"Hi Felix! I'm outside McDonald's. Can you see me?"

"I'm outside too, but I can't see you."

"Hang on. Which McDonald's are you at?"

"The one by the cinema, near the park."

A pause.

"Oh no. I'm at the one in Xiaobei. Shall we meet at the Garden Hotel instead?"

"Perfect. I'll see you there."

Eventually, a small blue Peugeot pulled up. Linda greeted him with an apologetic smile.

"Hop in," she called.

"No worries," Murray replied as he sat down. "It's all part of the adventure."

They drove towards Luhu Lake. Linda asked, "How are things at home?"

Murray groaned. "Not good. Jimmy's brother is still with us. Just sits there, living rent-free."

"In your head, Felix. Have you told Jimmy?"

"Not yet. I don't want to cause a scene, but it's getting ridiculous."

"Just be clear. Don't hint," she said.

Murray sighed. "Maybe I will, but I hate confrontation."

Rain fell steadily as they made their way to the lake, Murray holding his large umbrella over her. She spoke about her marriage, her disillusionment, and her work as a tour guide.

"I've been to the UK twice," she added. "But Kenya was the best. Ever seen lions two feet from your face?"

"That must have been scary."

"They came right up to the jeep. I froze."

"Did you think they'd jump in for a snack?"

Linda shuddered. "That thought crossed my mind."

Suddenly she stopped. "My bag. I left it on the front seat."

They hurried back to the car. Luckily, it was still there.

They talked more in the car until Linda said she had to pick up her sister. She asked him to call when he was free.

It was two weeks before they met again, this time at Zhongshanba. They went to a dim sum restaurant nearby. Murray was amazed at the size of the place.

"This is enormous," he said, surveying the sea of diners, mostly older folk.

They were shown to a table. Tea arrived, and Linda carefully washed the cups and chopsticks in hot water.

"Why do you do that?" Murray asked.

"It's the custom," she explained.

There was no English menu, so Linda ordered. The waiter handed them a checklist and a pencil. Linda ticked off the dishes before handing it back. Soon the food arrived.

It was traditional Guangdong dim sum, with seafood, meat, and vegetable dishes prepared in every way: steamed, fried, or baked. Dumplings, steamed buns, rice noodle rolls, and chicken feet featured heavily, alongside custard tarts, a popular favourite. There were steamed vegetables, stuffed peppers, soups, and sticky rice. Murray tried nearly everything.

"I'm still wary of chicken feet," he admitted.

"More for me," Linda said, grinning.

After the meal, she walked him to the metro.

"That was really good. I'm ready for a nap."

"I think you'd like to do this again," she said with a smile.

He returned home to the familiar sight of Jimmy's brother, sprawled out, completely at ease.

Later that week, feeling bored, Murray called Linda. They arranged to meet at 1 pm in Zhongshanba. This time she drove them to another dim sum restaurant, farther away, just as local and unpretentious.

They drank black tea in the sticky heat. Fans blew cold air from every corner. It was smaller than the last place, but the food was just as delicious. Once more, Murray ate until he was stuffed. Linda dropped him off at China Plaza afterwards.

Another two weeks passed before they met again. As usual, Linda chose the venue, knowing all the best spots. This time she took him to Liuhuaxiyuan Park for lunch.

"This is more than a restaurant," Murray said. The scenery was stunning, with rhododendrons, waterfalls, and a lake filled with lotus. Ponds were planted with aquatic flowers like lotus and blue bouffant. Thousands of dragonflies hovered over the water. In the exhibition halls, pavilion, and greenhouse, there were more than a thousand varieties of potted and subtropical plants.

"There's even a bird-watching teahouse," Linda said.

They wandered through the park after eating. Murray was particularly taken by a grove of oak trees.

"The English Queen, HRH Elizabeth II, planted those," Linda said. "Back in 1988. She was a sprightly sixty-something at the time."

"Are you serious?"

"She brought them from Windsor Great Park."

As they left, Linda mentioned she was heading to Nepal for a tour.

"I'll be back in nine days. Want to go to a hot spring when I return?"

Murray smiled. "If it gets me away from Jimmy's brother, count me in."

When she returned, they arranged to meet again. It was after dark when they met at Zhongshanba metro station. Linda arrived late, carrying a big orange tomcat.

"Felix, this is Tom. He's very sure of his place in the world."

Murray looked at Tom, and Tom looked at Murray. Neither said anything.

"Shall we go to the park?" Linda suggested.

"You brought your cat on a date?"

"He likes the park."

They sat on a bench while Linda stroked Tom and talked.

"Want to hold him?" she asked.

"I'd rather not. I'm allergic," Murray replied.

She frowned but continued showing him photos of Nepal, Dubai, and Kenya.

"Tom's a father cat," she said casually.

Murray blinked. "What?"

"A father cat."

"An unmarried or separated father?" he teased.

"He fathered three kittens this year, and four last year. The whole family lives with me."

He stared. "So you live with eight cats?"

"Nine. The mother too."

After Tom's full introduction, they walked back. Two little girls stopped to pet Tom on the way out. He froze, unimpressed.

"Not a people cat," Murray observed.

"Only the family. He's not used to strangers."

The next day, Murray sat at home, watching Jimmy's brother slumped at the computer, when his phone rang.

"Let's go to the hot spring on Monday," Linda said. "It'll cost about a thousand RMB. I'll drive."

"I'm with you," Murray replied immediately. He could not wait to get away from Jimmy's brother for a while.

They left early for Foshan. When they arrived, a long queue snaked outside the front door, but it turned out to be for checkout. They checked in straight away.

They had lunch, napped, then returned for dinner. That night they explored the hot springs.

"There are forty different pools," Linda said. "Varying temperatures, and some have minerals. Each one is supposed to do something magical."

"I just hope one of them wipes the memory of Jimmy's brother."

Under the glow of the new moon, they soaked, drank herbal tea, and lay on heated stone slabs. Murray watched the new moon overhead, so calm and distant, and felt the same peace settle over him.

"You're not bad company for someone who refuses to hold a cat," Linda said.

"I do like cats," Murray said. "But if I touch them, I get hives."

The next morning they enjoyed a buffet breakfast, soaked once more, then checked out. Back in Guangzhou, they had lunch. Linda glanced at her phone.

"Fiji next week," she said. "I've never been. I'm so excited."

"I'm happy for you," Murray said with a smile. "Just make sure you come back."

Two weeks passed. Murray heard nothing. When he guessed she must be back, he texted:

"Hi Honey. I guess you're home again? Can we meet for lunch? Can't wait to hear about your adventures!"

There was no reply for days. Then one afternoon she finally messaged:

"Hi Felix. I met a man on my travels. We've fallen in love. I'm sorry."

Murray read it twice, then a third time. The words stayed the same.

He put down his phone and looked across the room. Jimmy's brother was gone. Just an empty chair where the shadow used to sit.

He leaned back.

"Well," he said aloud. "I suppose everything's changed. Linda's found someone who bonds with the father cat. And Jimmy's brother has found a new home."

Luhu Lake

Joe McKenna was a dedicated hiker. Soon after arriving in Guangzhou, he began to map out a few routes. Initially, one of his regular walks was to Baiyun Mountain — in reality, more of a hill than a mountain. From the summit, the whole city could be seen on a clear day. There were three ways of ascending. The swiftest and most spectacular was by cable car, but you could also ride in an electric people carrier or walk.

When he was feeling energetic, he relished the climb. Usually, he went early in the morning. His route took him past the Aeon Mall, past the museum, along the side of a lake, and over several bridges spanning multiple highways.

To gain access to the "mountain", there was a small entrance fee. McKenna usually bought a bottle of water beforehand. There were always quite a few people going up and, even early in the morning, some coming back down. People carriers passed by, alongside police vans and trucks supplying the shops at the summit.

He usually walked at a good pace and overtook many of the more leisurely climbers. In the shade, it was cool, but sunlit patches were quite warm even in the early morning. At times it was hard going, but he found that periods of deep breathing helped. To keep focused, he would often count his steps. It irritated him when people cut across his path — something at which the Chinese were expert. He was forced to break stride and found it hard to regain momentum.

It took about half an hour to climb the mountain and it was rare for anyone to pass him out. There were usually many people milling about at the top, around the shops, cafes, restaurants, and stalls. In a nearby amphitheatre, various entertainers performed over the course of the day. At this time, walkers were entertained by a man with a flock of parrots. He had the birds lined up on perches, ready to perform avian stunts for their early morning audience.

McKenna seldom lingered there. Even though he sweated profusely, he would only rest briefly before setting off on the descent. Sometimes he met slow climbers whom he had passed on the way up. Going down wasn't as challenging as going up, but it was still trying, especially on steep inclines where the brakes had to be kept on constantly. At the bottom, there were always a few hawkers strategically located to tempt the thirsty with drinks and ice cream.

What he didn't realise for some time was that, on his way to Baiyun Mountain, he passed very close to the scenic Luhu Lake. He knew nothing of its existence despite its relative closeness to his apartment and its outstanding natural beauty. It never occurred to him to investigate the lake or its surroundings because it was concealed behind a thicket of trees.

He only discovered it thanks to Linda, a cat-owning tour guide, who drove him there on their first meeting. Linda had suggested a walk by the lake while they got to know each other. He barely saw the lake, being too busy listening to her stories about her divorce, her travels, and her two trips to the UK. But the glimpse intrigued him. As it began to rain, Linda suddenly stopped talking. Then, after a pause, she said, "I've left my bag in the car. And we have no umbrella." They hurried back.

The next time McKenna was back at the lake, it was with another friend, Sharon, who, like himself, loved walking. Again, it was raining, but this time it was late at night. He had a golf umbrella which covered the two of them as they did a full circuit of the lake. Although the lake was briefly illuminated by the odd flash of lightning, he couldn't see much. He did see that there was decking all the way round and that there were a few scattered restaurants, all shuttered at this time.

Their meandering walk lasted about two hours. Even though it was late, they weren't alone. A few fishermen were dotted here and there. Two security men were questioning a homeless man who had made his bed under a shelter. Further on, a middle-aged lady stood all alone on the path, texting.

Now that his interest had been aroused, McKenna started to walk round the lake regularly, mostly in the mornings. It took about eighty to ninety minutes. He developed a routine of buying dumplings and eating them as he walked. He would then purchase a small bottle of water further on. While the Baiyun Mountain walk was all about fitness and endurance, this walk was less strenuous and great for people-watching.

Sharon had shown him a shortcut to the lake. This route took him past Guangdong TV. On his way, he often saw two young kids playing outside the TV building. There was never any sign of a parent or minder. They always had a little black and white rabbit with them in a cage. Passers-by paid little heed to them as they sat there on the pavement, happily playing with their pet.

Just before the lake, McKenna had to pass the Guangzhou Museum of Art and the vast plaza in front of it. Entrance to the museum was free and the works included Chinese calligraphy, painting, and sculpture. He toured it once and, as well as the art, he was impressed by the beautiful courtyard garden at its centre, featuring koi ponds and sculptures.

Even early in the morning, there was a multitude of activities going on around the plaza. A large group of up to a hundred ladies did their daily yoga. Other smaller groups were engaged in various sports, exercises, and fitness routines. A constant stream of joggers and hikers passed by on their way to the lake.

One morning, as McKenna was passing along the road by the museum, he heard a woman singing and decided to have a look. A small crowd had gathered. As he approached, he caught sight of the singer. Beside her sat a one-legged man, his wooden leg prominently displayed, leaning against a wall. He could see the leg was decorated with green and gold strapping. On the ground before them lay a blanket-sized sign with some faded Chinese text on it.

After a brief stop, he continued with his walk. The duet were still there on his way back and this time the man was singing. A good few listeners remained, standing around them in a circle. The wooden leg had been thrown out onto the pavement and lay there, obstructing passers-by and forcing them out onto the road.

After crossing the plaza, it was only a short distance down to the lake. The cleaners and sweepers were always out early. Their job was to brush up the fallen leaves as well as the rubbish from the night before. Arriving at the lake, the sound of a saxophone could often be heard drifting across the water.

McKenna usually walked in a clockwise direction around the lake. Occasionally, he would walk in the opposite direction. Generally, the same people used the park every day at that time. However, if he walked one way, he met a totally different set of people than if he walked the other way. He went on to count the people walking each way. He found that 60% walked clockwise.

Sometimes he came across a small group of people playing a popular game using an extra-large shuttlecock. The aim was to keep the shuttlecock in the air for as long as possible, using only the feet. Some people just sat around on benches. Mothers watched over their children as they fed the black swans.

When he got as far as the saxophonist, McKenna figured he was halfway round the lake. The musician was ever-present on weekday mornings (Monday to Friday) and always had a small but loyal audience. He only played in short bursts. In between, he would leave the saxophone aside and sit down to chat with his listeners.

Further on, in a small clearing, a good number of bird fanciers assembled daily and each brought along his songbirds in a cage. The cages were hung in a row along a metal bar suspended about two metres off the ground. When the songbirds could be heard, it was a sign that the circuit of the lake was almost complete. The birds sang their hearts out to each other while their proud owners, mostly retired men, sat around drinking tea.

Sometimes he saw things at the lake which defied explanation. One morning he spotted a man walking a dog which was wearing a small jumper, as dogs do. It was also wearing a pair of denim jeans which looked very cute, except for the fact that the rear end had been cut out of them. He had often heard the expression about someone having "no ass in their trousers", but this looked grotesque.

Occasionally, he met people he knew — perhaps a group of students or a colleague. One day he met his student Chen, who was out walking with her mother. Her mother needed a break so the threesome sat down for a chat on a bench.

"Hi Chen. What brings you here?"

"Good morning, Mr Joe. My mother likes to come here for the fresh air."

"Are you not working?"

"No. I'm a lady of leisure."

"So what do you do with your time?"

"Well, apart from looking after my mother I do volunteer work at a hospital."

"That's very kind of you. What exactly do you do?"

"I help out at a traditional medicine hospital," Chen said.

"Do you do acupuncture?" he asked hopefully. "I have a problem with my back."

"Yes. Would you like to try? I can book you a free session."

Weeks later, he took her up on the offer.

Sometimes McKenna did the walk at night. There were still a lot of people about and the restaurants on the far side of the lake were fully illuminated, as was the bridge across the lake. But there was no birdsong and no saxophonist. They were of the morning.

At this time of night, the lake was a favourite haunt for courting couples. Here and there, pairs — in various poses — sat on benches. However, it wasn't all sweetness and light; on one occasion he saw a man sitting with his head in his hands while the lady was standing over him, giving him a very severe scolding.

In the evenings and at weekends, the plaza was extra busy. There would be hundreds of people everywhere, with traffic jams on all nearby roads. People played cards, mahjong, ping pong, and badminton. Crowds surrounded the various singers. Some just sat on benches, some talked in groups, and some sat alone. The more athletic walked, ran, or cycled. Children played alone or in groups while others drove around on mechanised pandas, bears, and lions.

The day before he left Guangzhou, McKenna decided to have one final walk around the lake. It was a grey, damp morning, but his spirits were high at the thought of a family reunion. As he was walking along, he met a man wheeling a bicycle backwards.

"That's China," he said to himself.

Green Tea and the Pink Panther

After living in China for a while, you know to expect the unexpected. One moment you're planning a simple errand, the next thing you're caught in a world of misinformation, bluff, bamboozlement, red tape, and unexpected cameo appearances by cartoon characters in the middle of a wild goose chase.

So it was, one fine morning, I was up early, a knot of anticipation and some anxiety already forming in my stomach. I had a simple goal: go to the post office and buy a postal order to pay for my new passport. 735 RMB (about £80) would be the total cost to cover the passport fee and postage. Straightforward, or so I thought.

I set off around 8:30 am, the city of Xianyang now settling again after the early morning rush. The No. 20 bus dropped me off on Wenlin Lu. I crossed the street and took the 13 bus a short distance along the main street. I alighted, crossed the street again, and marched into China Post.

On arrival, I encountered two ladies, one sitting behind the counter gazing into space and another sweeping the floor. As I would have expected, neither understood English, so I showed them the pre-prepared translation:

"I would like to purchase a postal order for 735 RMB."

The floor sweeper, surprisingly, was the first to respond. She leaned her besom against the wall and launched into a rapid stream of Chinese. Her gestures grew animated, pointing eastward down the street. Eventually, it dawned on her that I hadn't understood a word. She whipped out her phone, opened a translation app, and up came the message: Go to the Postal Savings Bank.

So off I went in the direction given. The sun was out. The air was warm. The birds were singing merrily. All in all, a beautiful morning. I figured this was a temporary blip — a minor inconvenience. It was about a ten-minute walk and, sure enough, the bank was where the lady had indicated.

But the moment I stepped inside, the familiar wall of incomprehension rose again. I held up my translation. Again, blank stares. A woman behind a teller window waved me away. Then a floor assistant, with a sweep of her arm, ushered me towards the exit. "Not here," her expression said. "Somewhere else." However, she did send me a location map on WeChat.

"Thanks," I muttered. My morning was turning into a treasure hunt.

I had to cross the street again and go down a side street which opened out into a big junction. There stood a China Post branch, as well as several banks. "Right," I thought, "Take your pick." I decided to try China Post first. I wandered in, and there were two ladies sitting behind desks. I approached one, my hope clinging by a thread. I showed her the translation. She looked at it, looked at me, then gave a dismissive wave. She called up another customer and blanked me totally. I pulled out my phone and rang my colleague Mr Qin. Could he rescue me? There was no reply.

Frustration simmered, threatening to boil over. I stood outside, down but not out, pondering my next move. I spotted a branch of ICBC, my own bank, just across the road. Inside, I was greeted warmly by two ladies.

"Can we help you?" one asked, offering some reassurance in a friendly voice. I launched into my tale. One of them immediately picked up her phone, dialling a friend for advice.

Just then, Mr Qin called back.

"Where are you? What's going on?" he demanded.

I recounted the entire morning's saga — the detours, the blank stares, the dismissals.

"Why don't you just use your VISA card?" he asked, incredulously.

"The Embassy won't accept credit card payments," I explained patiently.

"But why not?" he pressed, his voice suspicious. "What's the reason?"

"Mr Qin," I sighed, "if I knew, I wouldn't be here, would I? It's just... their policy."

Mr Qin then spoke to the lady who had been consulting her friend. Their conversation was long, punctuated by animated gestures. Finally, he came back to me.

"The ICBC cannot do this," he stated, his voice flat. "You must go to Bank of China."

The ICBC lady, ever so polite, echoed his words. "Yes, Bank of China. Around the corner."

"I know where it is," I replied, a bitter taste in my mouth. "I just passed it."

When I arrived, I found a lady inside who spoke good English, and after I had explained everything to her, she looked at me ruefully and said I should go to the International Section at their main office further up the road and that it was on the first floor. She walked out into the street with me and showed me which way to go, how far it was, and what the front of the building looked like. She wished me well and waved goodbye.

When I arrived, another small miracle: a lady who spoke excellent English.

"I want to buy a postal order," I declared.

"A postal order?" she asked, her expression rueful. "No, sir. Not here. You need to go to the main Bank of China branch, International Section. First floor."

She walked me outside, pointing the way, describing the building's façade, wishing me well. "Good luck!" she called.

It was a good walk along Renmin Lu. I spotted a McDonald's, a familiar refuge — coffee and a moment to refocus. The place had been renovated since I had last called. Now it had windows where you could see out but no one could see in. However, it appeared that a coffee machine wasn't part of their update. The coffee was burnt, bitter, and probably brewed several hours before. Needs must. I drank it anyway.

"What else can go wrong?" I wondered, staring into the murky depths of my cup. My previous visits to the Bank of China's International Section had never been a problem, thanks to a contact. But that contact was now gone. As an insurance policy, I decided to email Sunny at the Irish Embassy, asking for instructions in Chinese.

Half-fortified by the sickly brew, I arrived at the main Bank of China, just metres from McDonald's. I bounded up the stairs, only to be intercepted by a security man, a barrage of Chinese words greeting me.

"No Chinese," I said.

Then — hope! A teller behind a glass wall beckoned me over even though he was attending to one lady and had several more queueing. The security man gestured for me to go on ahead despite the queue.

"Come, come," the teller said in English.

Progress! He listened intently to my fragmented tale. I showed him the translation, but he barely glanced at it, his eyes fixed on the lady he was already serving. Stalemate.

Then, a stroke of genius! I'd call the Embassy again. This time, I got through to Sunny, but before she could help, the receptionist jumped in.

"Only China Post can issue a postal order," the receptionist stated, refusing to speak to the bank teller directly.

I hung up slowly.

"Sir?" said the teller as I walked off in a daze.

I limped out of there, shell-shocked and feeling like a member of Lord Edward's Army after being "sent homewards to think again." It must have been the effect of the coffee in the famous Scottish restaurant. Further refreshments were badly needed. King Coffee was nearby, and inside I sought some comfort and reassurance.

"I could do with a green tea," I said to the attendant.

This provoked no response. Déjà vu of a different colour. However, I now had my lateral, outside-the-box thinking cap on. There were two ladies sitting nearby, one nursing a large Pink Panther.

"Do you speak English?" I asked the Panther's mammy.

She smiled. "Yes! What can I do for you?"

"I want a green tea but the man doesn't understand English."

"Lu cha," she translated. The guy's eyes lit up — finally, a language he understood.

"That's 30 RMB," stated the lady.

The man took the money.

"Please, sit," she said, her voice gentle. "He will bring it to you."

I bowed and thanked them. I got my tea. Life was good again.

I was almost back to where I started. But things were looking up now. Then, a small victory: a reply from Sunny. Her email contained detailed instructions in

Chinese, again stressing that only China Post could issue the postal order. Surely, this time they would have to produce the postal order and accept my money.

It was noon when I crossed the road, back to the very China Post office where my odyssey had begun three hours earlier. The same two ladies. One behind the desk, silent. The other, still tidying. I triumphantly held up Sunny's email. She studied it meticulously, every character. But her gaze remained fixed on the paper. No movement towards the desk, no sign of action. My frustration bubbled.

"Look," I said, my voice rising, "I just need a postal order!"

Slowly, deliberately, she pulled out her phone. I braced myself. She typed. Then, she held up the screen. The translation appeared:

"China Post has recently been split into two entities. This office only deals with letters, parcels, and stamps. You must go to the Postal Savings Bank."

The second place I'd visited earlier.

Another circuit. My seventh attempt. I decided to take a bus, but to get to it I had to cross an intersection involving an underpass and an overhead footbridge. I later realised it would have been faster walking.

The Postal Savings Bank was bustling now, workers on their lunch break. There were no staff to be seen on the floor. I went up to a desk where someone was being attended and waited in turn. However, an old lady came in and walked in front of me. She engaged in a long discussion with the bank clerk. To my growing irritation, he ignored me completely. Another clerk walked by, lunch in hand, oblivious. The situation was now becoming critical. I was due at work soon.

Finally, I caught an unsuspecting bank lady as she was walking by and on her way into the back of the office. I showed her my email in Chinese. She looked at it but then took off into the back without comment or acknowledgement. I understood she was off to consult someone about the mysteries of the postal order.

I stood and waited, and waited. After a time, I sat down. The lady did re-emerge on a couple of occasions but paid no attention to me. I found it hard to keep cool.

Then, finally, a woman appeared. I waved my email in the air.

She vanished.

I waited.

She walked past me — twice — ignoring my existence. I snapped.

"EXCUSE ME!"

Heads turned. My voice could be heard throughout the office.

Suddenly, bank staff materialised from thin air. A desk was found. A seat was offered. I was in.

The clerk behind the glass smiled like nothing had happened. I was ushered to a desk. The lady behind the glass was another whom I had tried to engage with on my first visit but at that point didn't speak or understand English. Now she spoke perfect English, which I attributed to miraculous intervention by some newly-emerged deity previously unknown in these parts.

A chubby little male clerk now appeared. While I was dealing with the lady behind the glass, this guy was shovelling forms at me on the outside. All in Chinese.

"I don't understand Chinese."

He too then discovered he could speak English and pointed to the first field: "Name."

We played bureaucratic charades — me guessing each field, him muttering translations — passport, phone number, address.

After writing down the phone number, he rang me to check its authenticity. Then the passport had to be produced.

Another form. Another copy. Everything in triplicate.

"Why do you need all this?" I asked.

More typing. A document emerged. I was asked to check it, print name. Then I was led to the ATM.

"Oh, are we doing a transfer?"

"No. Just withdraw cash," said the clerk.

I withdrew the cash and returned to the desk with the money. I passed that through the looking glass, and then there followed a period of counting the money, examining the passport, checking the visa, and more typing. Then a white paper document was printed and passed out for me to sign. This was the thing I was looking for all day, I was quite sure of it. But she wasn't done yet.

"Two RMB fee," she announced.

I handed her 20 RMB and then there was a scramble to find change, but even that feat was now possible. I was handed out one part of the stamped document, my change, and my passport.

"Finished!" she declared, a triumphant smile lighting up her face.

I exited the bank holding that precious piece of paper as if I'd just retrieved the Ark of the Covenant.

Mission accomplished.

And I owed it all to Sunny, a psychic Pink Panther, and the power of raised voices in a room full of silent tellers.

Part Three

Motorbikes & Mekong

Online Teaching in Lockdown

Over the years, people occasionally suggested to me that online teaching could be the way to go. I always said I would not be interested and that it was a soulless experience which I would find excruciatingly boring and unfulfilling, to mention but two words. Then Covid happened, in Vietnam of all places.

In January 2020, I had just arrived in Ho Chi Minh City to work as an English teacher. It was a regular job in a regular environment, an English training centre. Kids would come to class in the evenings or at weekends, have their lessons, and go home.

For the first week, I was among a group of ten people who attended training at the company HQ. Then I was sent to a centre in Go Vap district. Kieran, the "Head Teacher," was Irish, so it was good for helping me settle in. I was only there two days before the Tet holiday kicked in and I was off for two weeks.

During those two weeks, I found an apartment, got organised there, and also had time to go to Vung Tau for a few days. This beach city was where a lot of American GIs spent their time off during the war of the 1960s. I liked it and resolved to return at a later date.

On my return to work, the world had changed. Covid-19 had appeared and was now the sole topic of conversation. We resumed our lessons, but many students were not turning up. This situation only lasted for a few days, during which time I observed a few colleagues' lessons and taught a few lessons to the small numbers of students who came. Then it was decided that offline lessons would be suspended altogether.

The next few days were chaotic. We were in an unprecedented situation. Everything was up in the air; the company was waiting to see what the government would do. Because of the uncertainty, they were not sure what strategy to adopt.

It was a surreal time. Schools had been ordered to close for two weeks initially. We were still going into work every day, but instructions were vague and constantly changing. Staff worried if they would get paid and whether they would be laid off. Vietnamese staff were already two months behind with salary, I learned later, although that was not Covid-related. A red flag I did not see.

As a further part of our training, we were expected to do a number of online courses. I did several of these at this time. There was personal stuff to attend to and forms to be filled in by my new landlord and then stamped at the police station. Immunisations had to be taken care of. It had suddenly dawned on me that hepatitis was something that could be picked up here, and there was also rabies and malaria to consider.

After some time, it was announced that the company would start online teaching and that it would be done from the centres. This was a new departure for all concerned and one I was not looking forward to. We would be using an app called Zoom that I had never heard of before, but which was to shoot to prominence worldwide over the next few months.

In the beginning, everything continued in a disorganised and haphazard fashion. We were still using the offline lessons, trying to squeeze 90 minutes' worth into 40 minutes online, which was difficult. After a few days of this, we got clearer instructions on what material from the regular lessons to use and what to omit. When we had got the hang of this, we were then instructed to work from home to cut down on close contacts. They did not want us getting Covid.

However, the lessons and the technology were often the least of our problems. Each class had up to 12 students and it was like a reality show in many ways. The teacher had to be able to see the students in their houses because it was necessary to make sure they were paying attention and not messing about.

However, it was not only the students who were visible. While lessons were in progress, there were often many distractions. Family members attended to their business in the background, dogs barked, and cocks crowed.

So there I was trying to teach a number of students, but I could not help seeing what was going on in their living rooms. Relatives just carried on their normal lives, unaware of the webcam. Family members were often to be seen sitting gossiping in the background. They cooked, cleaned, ironed, and washed themselves. People changed their clothes and sometimes wandered about naked or semi-naked without a care in the world.

Some of the students were very young and it was hard to keep them interested. It was like minding mice at the crossroads. Sometimes the parents would get over-enthusiastic and answer for or prompt the kids, often with wrong answers. Quite a few of the students used their phones to do the lesson and I once discovered a kid was taking the lesson whilst riding on the back of his father's motorbike. On another occasion, we were talking about birds and when I showed a picture of a particular bird a student shouted out that it was a "Gooster."

Students were assigned to groups but would change from one group to another without notifying us. They would change their names or have no name at all. They might appear on screen as Galaxy, iPhone, Samsung, etc. They would have different aliases which would change week to week. Then there were common names and one could have two or three Elsas, Marys, or Brians in the same class.

It was hard to know at times if kids were muting or unmuting themselves to avoid answering questions. It was difficult to tell if they could hear. Sometimes they might be speaking and I could not hear. Then there were the kids coming in and out constantly and having to be readmitted. You never knew whether it was faulty equipment or they were just messing.

On one occasion, I had a child in class who put a plastic bag over his head. It was funny at the time but dangerous. Another time, a student was attacked by his little brother during the lesson. One evening, a kid was shouting and roaring, writing on the screen, rolling around on a bed, then jumping all around the place doing contortions with not a parent to be seen. After all else failed, I had to eject him from the class.

"Today I had four classes in a row with a range of horrors. There were students who would not answer, students muting themselves, students taking a long time to answer and finally saying they did not know, people talking loudly in the background, people hammering and drilling in the background, dogs barking, cocks crowing."

"After several weeks of online teaching, feelings are hard to describe. It is not the horrible experience I thought it would be but it is different from face to face. There are surprises, some nasty and some nice. It definitely is not boring as you are constantly kept on your toes. Anything can happen at any time."

"Zoom is a strange app and no one had ever heard of it a few weeks before. Now it is everywhere without anyone having researched it or its effects. It is said that it can spy on people and feed information to Facebook. I do not know if that is true, but I do know that it sometimes cuts out and needs to be reloaded. It may even go down for a prolonged period of time. How much this is down to Zoom and how much to an overloaded internet is hard to know at this time."

Generally, feelings were running everywhere and in all directions during those days. There was no structure to life. There was no one to directly talk with, laugh with, cry with, or even fight with. Everyone was at least one step removed and it was like moving through a world of sounds and images, like involuntarily starring in a movie.

My age played into this too. As one gets older, one feels sidelined and irrelevant anyway. Young people pass us by as if we are not there and generally pay us little heed unless, of course, they want or need something. I had seen this in my training group. The others were all in their twenties except one slightly older lad, and he was the only one who talked to me on a conversational basis.

However, the online teaching was better than the alternative which would have been twiddling my thumbs. It kept some kind of vague shape on time, even though day seemed to pass to night and back to day again with very few signposts except the switching on and off of lights. Even sleeping was irregular and it was a matter of lying down when the mood took you. I found that worked for me anyway.

It did take over my life as I even found most of my dreams were about online lessons. Many different scenarios were explored, but the one thing about my dreams at the time was that they never ended. They did not have climaxes or conclusions. As one faded away, a new one rose to replace it.

I had a strange dream one night about my Head Teacher Kieran. In this dream, he was transformed into a pretty blonde lady and I had a big disagreement or misunderstanding with her. She looked at me so sadly as she castigated me for whatever sins I had dreamt of.

Every day was roughly the same and the only regular contact was with kids in class and the CMs (Teaching Assistants) at work who monitored the classes and dealt with problems on an ongoing basis. Teaching colleagues were all remote now and I only heard from them when there were major issues to be dealt with.

On top of the challenges we faced while teaching, when it came to payday we only got 30% of our salary and the rest was paid in dribs and drabs over the next few weeks. However, I carried on and most others carried on, although this was a second red flag which we all should have recognised. In fact, this situation deteriorated as time went on and came to a head later.

You were allowed to go to the supermarket and I sometimes went to the nearest, about fifteen minutes' walk away. There were people around but not many. Groups of unemployed Grab drivers sat on their bikes ready to answer calls at a moment's notice. The calls were scarce. Some lay on their bikes texting or sleeping. The few hawkers on the streets would look up hopefully at every passing face. The garbage collectors passed along picking up refuse and sorting it as they went.

Mostly, I had no errand to the supermarket at all, but I went for the walk. A man took your temperature at the entrance and offered hand sanitiser. Sometimes I might have a word with the girl who weighs the vegetables or the lady on the till. Other times, a customer would stop to chat, and they invariably wanted to know where I was from.

One day, I chatted to an old man who knew about Ireland and said he believed it to be a beautiful country. I was looking at saucepans, but I did not purchase. I then went in the food department to look around and came out with Jujubes, ham, yoghurt, dumplings, and a bag of onions even though I had no call for any of them.

"A friend back home emails me her story about dating. She met a man a while back (offline) through a mutual interest group for retired people. He asked her to go on a dinner date and the date was set but Covid intervened. They were overtaken by events and confined to their respective quarters. It is said that love will find a way, so they decided to resort to online dating and were preparing for their first Zoom encounter. She was getting ready as she wrote to me and was about to bathe and put on a nice dress, a necklace, and makeup. A bottle of Prosecco sat by the laptop on the table."

So days faded into nights followed by more days and nights. It was a world without end and without horizons. There was nothing to be said or done and news channels were at their wits' end on what to report as it all seemed to be Covid statistics, which had become monotonous and generally ignored. There was no other news. They had taken to playing endless repeats of nostalgia because there was no future imaginable. "The past is the only place that can be seen clearly as the now is somehow a kind of dreamland inhabited by masked ghosts and shadows who pass each other by, silently."

The online teaching was tough, but doing it without being paid was just too much to ask. At a certain point, I just resigned. I told them I could not do it any more. I had started working for a Chinese company, also online, and they did pay.

Sidestreets of Saigon

When you move to a new home, it takes time to develop habits. For a while, life can be a little unpredictable. You discover some new things you like. Other things that were routine in your last life now seem out of place. Additionally, it was the time of Corona (as it was known at the time).

My new residence was on the fourth floor of a brand-new building down a quiet side street. In fact, the building was not quite finished. I had a door which opened out into midair, but was assured that a balcony would be installed soon. Fortunately, the door remained permanently locked and without a key.

The building had a security man who seemed to be perpetually on duty. He sat in a front room downstairs watching all comings and goings. Nothing odd about that, one might say. But as time went on, I realised there was more to this man than met the eye. He sat on a stool by a desk which was more like a lady's dressing table. I say that because on that desk sat a small vanity make-up mirror. He seemed to spend a lot of his time admiring himself, adjusting and readjusting the mirror so he could look at himself from various angles. Not that there was anything wrong with that, but...

My street was more of an alley than a street. I lived about 200 metres from the main road. For most of the way, there were high walls on each side. Behind one wall was an army barracks, and on the other side were government offices. A short distance before my building, there were two or three coffee shops quite close together. They only seemed to open in the mornings.

Opposite where I lived was a temple. The monks there got the show on the road at about six in the morning. Although bells did ring and there was some chanting, they did not make a lot of noise, but occasionally it would wake me up. There were other ceremonies throughout the day, and it all rounded up in the early evening when they closed the gates. There was a dog in the monastery. He was very aggressive and ever ready for battle with any strange dog who happened to be passing.

As time wore on, I began to develop a loose schedule. Every weekday morning I would go out for coffee at about 10 o'clock. I came back for lunch and then rested until it was time for work, about 4.30 pm. The weekend was different. I spent most of my time at work, teaching kids.

I was off all day on Mondays and Fridays. On these days (and occasionally on others), I went to the supermarket. To get there involved navigating through a maze of side streets and alleyways. On this occasion, as I exited the building, a cur sat chewing a cigarette butt on the street outside. Another lay prostrate on its belly with its head resting on the road. A man carrying a long pole cycled past. I wondered if he was practising for some new Olympic sport. A cycling pole-vaulter.

These backstreets were about two metres wide at maximum and often a lot narrower. My street was actually a little broader, but cars struggled to negotiate it, especially if there were other vehicles parked. About 50 metres past my building, there was a junction. Beyond that, all the streets leading off it were too narrow for cars.

Most of the traffic consisted of motorbikes, including Grab drivers picking people up and dropping them off. Sometimes the garbage collector came along. He drove an adapted motorbike towing a high-sided trailer. He was accompanied by another person inside the trailer who tramped the rubbish down to maximise the load. There were also a couple of big, oversized Santa Claus-type sacks tied on behind the trailer. These held recyclables like plastic bottles and cardboard.

Once past my building, along the first section of road, were mostly private residences where the people lived behind high gates. Sometimes you could see through the bars of the gates into the houses. You might hear a dog barking at passers-by. Some gates were left open if there was a business or apartments within.

There were two visible commercial premises, one a shop selling art supplies and another selling paintings and sculpture. Both were always busy. One of them ran art courses as well. People could be seen sitting around in a group, drawing and painting. In the other place, the sculptor was always at work.

Sometimes a car drove as far as the crossroads and then had to turn and retreat. Some people did drive up and park if they were visiting someone in the locality. There was a kind of little square there with a few small shops and cafes.

After a while, I got to know a teenager who worked as a dishwasher in one of the cafes. This lad had a learning disability and always shouted out when I passed. Of course, I returned the greeting. There were usually a few people around, sitting outside the various residences, shops, and the cafe. Most were retired people, and many of them also greeted me as I passed. At times, young people hung around there too, especially during Corona, when schools were closed.

Next door to the cafe was some kind of pre-school or kindergarten based in the living room of a house. Glancing in, it looked like there were up to 20 kids in there. They sat at two long tables with two or three teachers in attendance. These kids seemed very diligent and well-behaved. Every time I walked past, they were deeply engrossed in their books.

Whichever way I went, I had to negotiate a maze of very narrow streets. On this route, the next alley was about thirty metres long. On the left was a row of houses. On the right was a wall enclosing someone's garden.

In the evening, a middle-aged lady and her daughter opened a mobile restaurant along the wall. This consisted of a cart containing the food, with a big rice cooker sitting on a table nearby. They also brought a few tables and chairs to seat customers. The lady always greeted me, but the daughter just worked away with no sign of recognition.

After passing the caterers, facing me on the next corner was the front door to a house. Sometimes the residents could be seen inside doing all the things people do in their abode. There were kids in this house and they often appeared to be clambering over motorbikes (people take their bikes indoors when not in use). Sometimes the father could be seen lying in a hammock watching TV.

I took a left turn there and travelled about another twenty metres to another junction and turned right. At that junction, there were a couple of businesses advertised, but their signs were in Vietnamese. I did not have a translator to enlighten me.

In fact, these backstreets were crammed with all kinds of residences and businesses. Some operated as both. There were small barber shops, hairdressers, nail bars, manicurists, beauticians and various others offering specialist treatments for ladies.

My hair was getting long. On this particular day, I was in no hurry, and so I decided to stop at a barbershop. Inside, I was confronted by a neat little man with shoulder-length hair. A girl was attending to another customer beyond. I was ushered into a chair next to the door and the man got to work. After he had finished cutting my hair, he asked if I wanted a shave and I said no. He then asked if I wanted my ears and nose done. I said yes.

By this time, the girl had finished with the other customer, and she took over. I was brought to another chair and laid out horizontally. Not only did she cut the hair inside my ear, but she started to fish out lumps of wax. My ear must have been like a mini beehive. She spent 15 minutes on it. Then she did the same on the other ear.

She then invited me behind a partition. I was laid down again on a chair with my head backing onto the sink. She washed my face and head with cold water. Then she rubbed oil into my face and head, washed it all off and repeated. This time she gave me a full facial massage followed by a head massage. She rinsed me off again before a final massage and yet another rinse.

That was not the end. She put me sitting up in the original chair where I had sat when I came in about 70 minutes before. There she gave me a final rubdown. I was not sure how much this might cost. It ended up at about 160,000 Dong or €6. Off I went, a little bemused but well-groomed.

In one of these alleyways lived a stout little woman with two dogs. One was a small yellow and white mongrel. The other was not big but, like his mistress, he was sturdily built. He looked like some breed of bulldog. This dog was very ugly and appeared to suffer from respiratory difficulties. Any time I passed, he was panting and his tongue was hanging out. When it was very hot, he sat on his backside close by a portable fan positioned right next to an illuminated Buddha.

Through time, I discovered that there were actually two fans in that lady's front room, one on either side of the shrine. Owner and dogs sat there like those in a colder climate would sit at a fire. At night, there was an eerie glow from the shrine. To the passer-by, it was like looking into some kind of doggie limbo.

In the daytime, the dog owner was always busy fussing and cleaning around the house and spent a lot of time at her potted plants on the wall outside, ably assisted by the senior dog when he had the energy. The smaller dog was a little timid. While the work was going on, it usually stood in the doorway looking up and down the alley. The lady weeded and watered constantly. She kept the street outside her house in pristine condition, brushing regularly and even washing and scrubbing it last thing at night.

It would also appear that the lady had a family or at least a daughter. At weekends, a bicycle was often seen parked outside strapped to a drainpipe. A young lady could be seen within, looking very much at home among the dogs, the fans, the mother and the Buddha.

Most of the houses on this street had dogs, although some were only seen occasionally. Two doors up from the busy lady lived a small cream-coloured poodle that sat perpetually looking out on its known world. Its coat always looked the worse for wear, like a mat that had been washed too often.

While there were some pedigree dogs like the previously mentioned bulldog and poodle, mutts seemed to be popular. Most dogs were kept indoors, although sometimes they sat on the street outside. In these situations, they were usually restrained. People often washed their dogs out on the street, using a dish of soap and water. After a good scrubbing, they then hosed them down.

Across the road from the bulldog and the lady was a small workshop in the front room of a house. They always had a stack of garments on the floor. They packaged them up into plastic bags and presumably shipped them out to shops. On closer inspection, you could see people working away down the back, sewing and stitching. I had an idea they were making pyjamas. They beavered away all day in there and then in the evening everything was cleaned up, garments bagged and the floor swept, ready to go again the next morning.

Next door to this was a house outside which sat two men on wicker chairs. They drank beer, smoked cigarettes and saluted all passers-by. In the evenings, they were joined by several other men to sit around chatting and playing cards. There were cats in that house and in the house beyond it too. These cats watched passers-by nervously, often running indoors at any sign of humans approaching.

After another left turn sat a house on the next corner where they made all sorts of things. The alley was wider there and once I saw a row of freshly made uniforms hanging on chairs outside. On another occasion, they were making a coffin. This coffin was a yellow colour. What struck me was the painting of the Last Supper on the side of it, in colour and done very professionally. Apt or what?

At that point, one must turn right and immediately afterwards there was a restaurant which only opened in the morning. It seemed to do very good business and always had a lot of people inside as well as motorbike delivery men queuing up outside to carry orders off to remote customers. The ladies there always had a friendly greeting, although I never had the pleasure of dining there.

Just before coming out onto a main thoroughfare, there was a nail salon. Several young girls were employed there. Looking in, you could see their lamps in the darkened room. Clients sat on a row of chairs. The workers scarcely seemed to move as they focused on their delicate task in the shadows.

After that, it was back out into the world. A broad bustling street with big stores, hawkers, taxis, trucks, buses and, further along, my usual destination, the supermarket.

The Long An Bus

It was 2020. I was working in Long An province. About once a month I would travel into Saigon. The journey from Tan An City to Saigon took about 90 minutes. Buses ran regularly to the extent that you did not need to check a timetable. Just arrive and there would always be a bus waiting. They departed about every 15 minutes.

The Long An terminus was always busy, with up to 20 buses there at any given time. I rode there on my motorbike and parked in the station, which was very convenient. The parking attendant issued a ticket and wrote something in chalk on the passenger seat.

The buses were a sky-blue colour, and most of them had seen better days. Inside these boneshakers, legroom was at a minimum. For locals, it was generally tolerable, but for a tall person it was uncomfortable. I always sat near the back. Sometimes the air conditioning did not work. The one thing that always worked was the horn. The driver blew it constantly to warn errant bike riders who might stray into his path.

Before setting off, the bus was visited by an assortment of hawkers and pedlars of various goods, from orange drinks to French baguettes to bags of cooked quail eggs. There were also people selling lotto tickets. In fact, every time the bus stopped, more vendors got on. Sometimes the bus waited while they did their business, and other times they got on at one stop and off at the next.

The driver always started the engine five minutes before leaving. At the appointed time, the bus set off at a snail's pace. When it reached the gate, it stopped. The hawkers got off and the conductor got on. Every bus had a conductor who worked closely with the driver. Some conductors stationed themselves up beside the driver at the front door. Others positioned themselves at the second door halfway down the bus. Sometimes you would not even notice their presence until they started collecting fares. This did not usually happen until about 10 minutes into the journey. Neither driver nor conductor wore a uniform. Drivers were generally men, but conductors were of both sexes.

Such was the situation this morning as our man stationed himself in the seat beside the side door. Progress was slow as the bus drove through the city. It had to stop to pick up both parcels and passengers. This was where the conductor came into his own, hopping off to carry heavy luggage on or off the bus. There was also the matter of helping people who were a bit stiff. He would take them by the arm and guide them up or down the steps.

On this bus today, the conductor also had a push button to open and close the side door. It looked like the driver did not let anyone or anything through the front door at all unless a package was being collected. In that case, the conductor would get off, pick the package up and drop it in beside the driver. If it was a bulky parcel, then it was brought in through the middle door and deposited there, in a space between the seats.

The bus had many stops in the early part of the journey. Stop was not always the appropriate word. Sometimes it paused more than stopped, especially if the boarding or alighting traveller was young and light on baggage. In that case, the bus just slowed down. The passenger hopped on or off while the bus was in motion. Of course, if there were multiple passengers or heavy luggage involved, there would have to be a full stop to load or unload. The conductor was kept busy dealing with voyagers, suitcases and parcels.

At the first stop, five hawkers got on and wandered up and down the aisle promoting their wares. Among the goods on offer were boiled eggs and bottled water. One man in a yellow and black striped jumper came on and did a presentation to the captive audience. He was up near the front, but from what I could see he was selling some kind of razor-cum-back scratcher. The bus waited for some time while he went through his routine. Two of the passengers then made a purchase.

At the next stop, four salespeople got on. This time they were selling different goods than the last visitors. There were chicken pieces, fruit, bread and cakes on offer this time. Again, there was quite a lengthy wait before the bus set off again. One woman even had time to get off and go into a roadside store to do her shopping.

There were also mystery stops at certain buildings. The conductor would go inside and spend a couple of minutes before reappearing. It was not clear what went on in these places. He brought nothing in or out.

As we emerged from the city, the bus stopped less often. We were travelling along a broad road, but not the motorway. All along this road were shops, cafés and restaurants. Places for the weary traveller to literally lay his head. These establishments had rows of hammocks where travellers could rest up for a while.

Along the route there were many outlets selling heavy machinery like diggers, tar spreaders, steamrollers and so on. There were even more selling tractors of all sizes and descriptions. These ranged from John Deere to Massey Ferguson to Ford, down to very small homegrown tractors. Then there were those selling other farm implements like rotavators, grubbers, ploughs, combines, rice harvesters and whatever else was needed for local agriculture and horticulture.

Another feature of travelling this road was the number of mansions springing up here and there. Some were already lived in, with more under construction. No expense was spared. Ostentation was the name of the game. There were temples and churches too, one grander than the next. Some of the temples flew swastika flags on top of their twin spires. The swastika is a Buddhist symbol which the politically correct people have not had an opportunity to deal with yet. The temples and monks are closely aligned with the Communist Party. In fact, the party pays for the upkeep of the temples and the monks' salaries.

Then there was the big field full of concrete animals. The giraffe stood out, towering above all the others. There was also an elephant and many other natives of the savannah, not to mention cattle and horses. The animals were all in their natural concrete state, that is, grey. Perhaps when they got an owner they were given a new coat of paint. They were life-size and must have been very weighty. No danger of theft.

As we drove through the countryside, there were occasional roundabouts, but it was mostly a straight run. Passengers continued to get on and off, but a lot less frequently. A few miles out of Tan An, a woman boarded. She did not look comfortable at all and sat fidgeting. The next stop was on a garage forecourt. The woman decided she needed to go to the toilet. While we were there, the conductor got off and did some stretching exercises on the tarmac in front of the bus. The woman did not re-emerge for about fifteen minutes.

As the bus came into Saigon, there were more stops as people started to get off. Again, for young and fit people the bus only slowed down and they jumped off while it was in motion. Older passengers and those with baggage did deserve a proper stop, and the conductor made sure they all got off safely. He was also called on to retrieve luggage from the hold underneath if it was bulky or heavy.

Passengers had to run another risk getting on and off if the bus could not pull in close to the kerb. Motorbikes were liable to come speeding up the inside as people were getting down from the bus. The conductor made sure the coast was clear before allowing passengers to alight.

Cholon Bus Station is in the southern suburbs of Saigon. It is much bigger than the Tan An depot, with services to cities nationwide. When the bus arrived, there was an army of motorbike taxi men waiting to offer their services. They crowded around the door trying to outbid and outshout each other, making it difficult for passengers to disembark.

This depot is near Saigon's Chinatown. Just outside the main gate is a fruit and vegetable market. Further along, live chickens, ducks and many other smaller fowl were on sale. These birds were kept in cages, stacked on top of each other. I fought my way through the massed ranks of those offering all kinds of sales and services. When I got as far as the gate, I ordered a Grab car and waited to be picked up and brought to the city centre.

On the trip back the pattern was similar. One minute the bus was half empty. Only women on board. Just as it was about to pull out, there was a rush of smokers who had been enjoying their last-minute cigarettes. All male. Vietnamese women do not smoke. Again, there were many stops until we cleared the city. At the first stop, the bus waited a long time even though there were no peddlers. The second stop was at a petrol station. A few passengers got on, as well as two sales ladies, one dealing in bottled water and the other selling lotto tickets.

The bus was soon fairly full. On the seat by the side door, an old woman sat in a Buddha-like pose. She greeted everyone as they boarded. During the journey, she carried on talking. Another lady was carrying a little brown bird in a plastic bag. It kept chirping and she tried to cover it with her hand to quieten it. All those in the aisle seats sat with their legs crossed, one foot on the floor and one in the air. The dangling foot was invariably bare, sandal on the floor.

At one of the last stops before we left the city, the bus again halted for a lengthy spell. Two middle-aged ladies sat peeling pineapples in front of a motorcycle repair shop. Inside this workshop, a thin man in a long white coat was carefully examining a motorbike. Three girls who looked like models got on. Unlike most passengers, they carried no baggage.

One hawker boarded the bus. She was selling bread rolls and two or three people purchased. When she had her business done and left the bus, we set off again. Just before we reached the highway, we passed under a flyover. Underneath, protected from the sun and the rain, a few vendors were selling their wares. There were various caged animals and birds for sale, including chickens, ducks, puppies and kittens.

Once we were on the highway, the bus made good progress. About halfway to Tan An we came on the scene of an accident. As the bus slowed down, I looked out to see what was happening. The bus was in the outside lane. On the side of the road was an ambulance with lights flashing and its siren blaring. A crowd had gathered around it.

Most people on the bus were drawn to the commotion on the roadside. I happened to look the other way. A man lay spreadeagled in the central reservation, unseen or unnoticed by anyone. His face seemed badly damaged, mutilated. There was blood everywhere. He could have been dead. The ambulance crew were obviously attending to other injured people. Perhaps there was so much traffic they had not seen him out there. The traffic did not stop. The bus kept moving.

The rest of the journey was uneventful. More of the same. Mansions, garden centres, furniture shops, factories, temples and warehouses. On arrival in Tan An, there were several motorbike taxis waiting, not so close nor as numerous as in Saigon, but still advertising themselves.

I picked up my bike and checked out. The man looked at the mark on the passenger seat, took my ticket and charged accordingly.

Part Four

After the Long Road

The Happy Inca

It was a Monday morning in June. Mark Jordan was on his way to a new job in Brixton. His fifth job in a month. A whirlwind of calamities had led him here, several competing thoughts running through his head as he walked through the gate.

"Here we go again!"

"Déjà vu?"

"Same old, same old."

"Maybe something different this time?"

The interview process had been brief. He had seen an ad in the evening paper and rang the number.

"Hello. I saw your ad. You are looking for bricklayers?"

"Yes, we need bricklayers. You got experience?" Graham's voice was clipped.

"Yes. Over twenty years," Mark replied.

"Very good. Can you start Monday?"

"I'll be there."

"£120 a day. Ask for Eric when you arrive."

He then gave directions to the job.

On arrival, the security man directed him to the office. Several other newcomers were already there waiting to be processed. Introduction then induction. Mark waited in line. He had time to have a good look at his new employer. The face of Gori Developments was a swarthy little fellow, fortyish, balding and, judging by his accent, obviously not English. He spoke in a nervous and excitable way, yet he had a friendly demeanour.

When it was Mark's turn, Eric barely looked up from his clipboard.

"Trade?"

"Brickie."

"Right. Bob the foreman will take care of you."

He was put to work with the other new recruits. Bricklayers usually worked in pairs, and Mark was partnered with Tom, a Cockney and a joker. The new men joined a team of Ukrainian labourers who had been on site for some time preparing the ground.

The neighbourhood was a hive of activity. Eric's housing project was one of several new developments along a main thoroughfare, each with its own army of workers. Across the street was a primary school with children, parents and teachers continually coming and going. To add to the chaos, British Gas were digging a trench down the middle of the road.

Trucks, dumpers, forklifts, diggers, rock breakers and jackhammers interacted with prams, buggies, babies, mothers and a fair scattering of dogs. The air was filled with the sounds of drilling, hammering, engines revving, kids playing, babies crying and dogs barking. Eric's men were sometime actors, sometime spectators as the various scenes played out.

On site, the Ukrainians did most of the donkey work. Like all immigrants from Eastern Europe, they tended to work as a team. They habitually followed each other around like a procession of ducks. Their leader, Andras, was a thin, blond, languid-looking fellow. He had a reasonable command of English and relayed Eric's instructions to the rest of his men.

Andras had recently been joined in London by his girlfriend Maria.

"Before Maria came, I save fifteen thousand. Shop at Lidl," Andras sighed, shaking his head. "Now? Harrods. Savings gone. But..." He smirked. "She really is beautiful!"

Vlad the Inhaler had formerly been a tank driver cum mechanic in the Red Army. He was called upon any time a machine broke down. While his English was limited, he had a deep understanding of mixers, dumpers and concrete saws. He smoked like a train. The rest of the Slavic cohort spoke no English, kept their heads down and worked quietly and anonymously.

Mark found himself among a team of eight bricklayers and four hod carriers, initially strangers to each other, but not for long. Those in the wet trades were always brothers in arms. In truth, a motley crew of tall-story tellers, shape-shifters, dreuths, wanderers, philanderers and the odd family man.

The mild-mannered foreman, Bob, was a rarity in the building industry. He valued tidiness and knew how to plan and organise. Brickies received the right materials in the right place at the right time. His standard advice to the men was to keep a tight line and ensure the bubble was always in the middle. After that, he left them to it.

One of the highlights of Mark's first day was the rise and fall of a newly recruited hod carrier. He tried to show off, running hither and thither with hodfuls of bricks and mortar. But he over-extended. By lunchtime, he was out on his feet.

"Look at him!" Tom cackled as the poor lad stumbled about.

"Gonna feel that tomorrow!"

From that day on, he was the butt of many jokes, immortalised as Superhod. The Ukrainians enjoyed his rapid demise. They were used to working away slowly and steadily and didn't take kindly to anyone trying to show off.

There was no canteen on site. Some workers brought packed lunches and others went outside at break times. There were two local options, Bonnie's Café or the Inca Stores. The former was round the corner on the next street and usually referred to as The Greasy Spoon. It was aptly named.

From time to time, the workers went to Bonnie's for   breakfast. Tom was greatly taken by Myrtle, the dark-haired waitress. He ogled the girl mercilessly.

"Myrtle makes my day. Those tight jeans really show off her bum."

"A labour of lust, Tom?" said Mark, laughing.

Mark had his eye on the tall blonde at the till.

"Wonder what her name is?" he said, gesturing towards her.

"Dunno, but why don't you ask her?" Tom teased.

Unfortunately for Mark, that was as far as it went. He never managed to take that step.

Apart from the two ladies, there wasn't much else about Bonnie's to be enthused about. Favoured customers were always served immediately while others had to wait. Going there was always a gamble. The food was middling at best.

"Burnt sausages and runny eggs today?" Mark looked ruefully at his plate.

"Chef's special," Tom said, pulling a face.

The Inca Stores was the other option. It was just along the road from the site. While it had an exotic name, it was also notable for its window display, a multitude of geraniums in a rainbow of colours. Mark never forgot his first visit to this strangely named retail outlet. As he entered, a bell rang. Away at the back of the premises, a dog barked. Standing facing him across the counter was a formidable-looking figure. A tall heavyweight with long grey hair and a freckly face. Obviously the proprietor.

The owner introduced himself as Fernando. He was from Peru. That explained a lot.

"Ah! New recruits for Eric?" Fernando boomed.

"Welcome, my friends!"

"Cheers," Mark said, spotting the Chunky KitKats.

"Eric is good man. You will enjoy working here!"

"And his partner?"

"Graham? Don't know him really."

The one downside to the Inca Stores was that it didn't serve hot food. However, sandwiches were available, as were bread, milk and cigarettes. There were some sweets, chocolates and biscuits. For Mark, the saving grace was the presence of the Chunky KitKats.

Yet this wasn't just a common or "garden" corner shop. As well as geraniums, groceries and tobacco it stocked a collection of teddy bears, a wide variety of trinkets from South America and a range of Tupamaros posters. Mixed in with these was an assortment of old Jimi Hendrix memorabilia.

While there was pandemonium in the street outside, the Inca Stores was an oasis of calm. The jovial Fernando knew and had time for all of his customers. Most of the building workers visited daily, as did the gas men, the kids from the school and the local housewives. His regulars often greeted Fernando with "Buenas Días" and that thrilled him hugely.

Because of his jovial disposition, the Peruvian was widely known as "The Happy Inca." His wife was Spanish and of a similar build to himself. She seldom spoke but, like her husband, she wore a perpetual smile. They lived at the back of the shop. There were no known children.

Customers confided in the Inca. The local women loved him. Blacks, whites and Asians all shared their innermost secrets. He had a word for everybody and had great empathy for the construction workers. While Mark ritually bought a Chunky KitKat, his mate Tom was addicted to Wagon Wheels, which he referred to as the biscuits with the see-through chocolate.

On the job, Eric would sometimes stand silently watching the bricklayers. Listening. Sometimes he would join in. When ladies were mentioned he would get very animated, spitting on his hands and rubbing them together.

Tom would start it. "I can't wait to get my hands on that Myrtle."

"You think she's beautiful, Tom? You should see the ladies in my country!"

"I'd say you've had plenty of experience, boss," retorted   Tom.

Eric would laugh, hopping from foot to foot.

While Eric was extrovert and popular with all the men, his partner Graham was a dour, colourless character. Reputedly very rich, and mean with it. He seldom visited the site and, when he did, he didn't engage with the men, unless it was strictly necessary.

It was said that Graham had found his wife online. Occasionally she went to visit her family in the Philippines. Rumour had it that Graham wouldn't drive her to the airport. He sent her by public transport in order to save money.

Tom loved to stir it. "They say Graham's wife was a mail-order bride."

"How much d'you reckon he paid?" Mark asked.

"Maybe ten grand?" piped up Superhod.

"You would hardly get a woman for that. I'd say twenty!" claimed Tom.

The payment was the source of ongoing speculation among the workers. Vast sums were bandied about, without a shred of evidence.

The site had many visitors, from building inspectors to architects to delivery men. One day a very shifty-looking character stopped by. Eric was waiting for him. He got out of his car and looked around furtively before opening the boot. It contained all sorts of power tools. There was much haggling before Eric eventually parted with money. The goods were then unloaded by the Ukrainians and taken to the store. The bricklayers could see the whole transaction from above.

"Dodgy gear," Tom muttered. "Bet it's all nicked."

"It's not the first time that guy has called," asserted Superhod.

Because Graham was seldom around, Eric always had to face the music when problems arose. The Clerk of Works was a constant thorn in his side. There were sometimes heated exchanges with neighbours over parking. Vandalism was an issue at weekends. When it all became too much for Eric, he retreated to the Inca Stores. One day Mark and Tom were in the shop when the topic of Eric arose.

"Why does Eric always visit at quiet times?" Tom enquired.

Fernando leaned over the counter and spoke in a low voice.

"You know Eric has a lot of things on his mind."

"We all have a lot of things on our minds."

"But Eric has so many responsibilities, so many targets to meet, so many deadlines. A lot of people to keep happy."

"So?"

"He comes here for counselling and advice. I provide him with special tablets to settle his nerves."

"Really. Are you joking?" said Mark.

"I'm serious. Of course he wouldn't want the workers to know."

"I suppose not," admitted Tom. "Don't worry. The secret is safe with us."

Whatever about Eric's problems, the brickies had to carry on, laying brick after brick after brick. They didn't allow the tedious nature of their work to bother them. They were multitaskers. There were constant debates, discussions and arguments. The usual topics were football and girls. As the building grew they had a bird's-eye view of the world above and below. Concorde was often seen and always heard. Nothing in the street escaped their notice, including the movements of the Inca.

First thing in the morning, Fernando walked his dog, a medium-sized beast of creamy colour and uncertain pedigree. Tom defined it as a doggy mixture. Man and dog would walk across the road to a little park. The Inca sat on a bench while the pooch did its business under the weeping willow that overhung Jeffra Parade.

After their walk, the two of them would go off to the market in Fernando's van. This yellow Bedford of 1970s vintage wasn't running well. Fido always sat upright in the passenger seat. The van seemed to go in fits and starts, jolting Fernando and his canine companion up and down in sync with it as it rumbled along.

Around one o'clock every day, after he had returned to base, the Inca would amble down the street with a potted geranium under each arm. His wife and the dog minded the shop. He greeted everyone as he passed. About an hour later he would come back empty-handed. There was great interest in the destination of the plants. The mystery fuelled endless speculation with all clues carefully dissected and analysed.

"Where do you reckon they go?" Mark asked. Typically, Tom's imagination ran wild. "They're for a fancy woman," he declared.

"They could be for a rabbit breeder," Bob guessed.

"Health food shops use them, don't they?" Superhod   offered. Eric shrugged. "Some bakeries use the leaves to flavour rhubarb tarts."

"Maybe he delivers them to another shop or garden centre," proffered Mark.

While everyone was dying to know, no one ever asked the obvious question.

While Fernando was generally a jovial character, he also had a serious side. One day he spoke of his past. He had been a rebel in his home country. Eventually, he was forced to flee.

"This guy was a close friend," Fernando said, pointing to a poster of a man in a sombrero, "first revolutionary leader in South America. Before Che. Executed in front of his wife."

Tom was there just listening. He didn't involve himself in serious conversations. To lighten the mood he asked, "Fernando, do you like the new TV series, Big Brother?"

"Yes, my wife and I have started to watch it. That Nick guy is so sneaky?"

Soon the Peruvian was his smiling self again and all was well with the world. Another customer entered, the bell rang, the dog barked and the men headed back to work.

Inevitably, all good things come to an end. The job ended and it was time to move on. The bricklayers finished early that day and they all called on Fernando to say their last goodbyes.

Fernando's eyes glistened. "My friends! You take these." He presented each of them with a Chunky KitKat.

As the redundant workers headed for the tube, Fernando set off on his daily march of the geraniums, still with no one any the wiser as to their destination.

Lonely Hearts

It was midsummer and he was kicking his heels. Off work for three months. Wondering what to do with himself. After a non-eventful couple of weeks, he decided to try online dating. It was a means of passing the time, and he might even get lucky. That was how he came to meet #DramaQueen.

At first, their exchanges were tentative. Neither gave much away. He did learn she was in Coleraine, and he told her that he was in Belfast.

"I passed through Coleraine on a train last week."

"Pity I missed you. LOL. I live about five minutes from the railway station. You could have dropped in for coffee."

"Would it be a strong brew?"

"It could be adapted to taste!"

"You sound very accommodating."

"Within reason!"

"One can't get carried away."

"Every day is a school day."

"Well, most days. Do you work full-time?"

"No. I have two part-time jobs. I teach Speech and Drama and I am also a personal stylist."

"I'm an ESL teacher. I'm off until September."

"I teach privately, so don't finish until the end of next week."

"Do you work days or evenings?"

"Evenings are sacred. I work days."

"I could come your way next week if you had a free day."

"I only work a full day Monday and Thursday. The other days are my own. As you have already said, I am accommodating. And I only work a few hours at my fashion job."

"Well then, how about next week? I'm away to a party at the weekend but should be recovered by Monday. Maybe Tuesday or Wednesday?"

"Leave it with you."

"I can give you my number if you want to use WhatsApp."

They began to text on WhatsApp. She liked the chit-chat. He didn't. He wanted to arrange a meeting and leave it at that. She wasn't really happy with short exchanges. She wanted to get to know him better before meeting. To him, she appeared to be a person who hadn't much going on in her life.

While she wanted to find out more about him, he was happy to wait until they met. He would have plenty to say then. He preferred to talk face to face. Trying to get that across to her proved difficult. He would tell her he was going outside, going shopping or going to visit his brother. She still wasn't happy about how he terminated their exchanges so abruptly.

That weekend, he went off to a wedding in Fermanagh. They did exchange a few messages while he was gone. Each time, he had the feeling that she was ready for a long bout of texting. There was always another question. It made him feel uncomfortable, like he was being interviewed, even quizzed. He always ran out of things to say. She thought he was being cagey, hiding something.

Monday came, and with it more texting. He was consciously polite. After the preliminaries had been gone through, he asked about setting the time and place for a meeting. She didn't reply to his question.

"How was your weekend?" she enquired.

"Good, but I'm tired today."

"Was it worth it?"

"Of course. I met up with people I hadn't seen in a long time. I drank too much."

"I don't drink at all. Are you a big drinker?"

"Not really. Just on special occasions."

"I hope not. I was brought up in a pub. I saw the effects of alcohol every day."

Once more, he felt she wanted a prolonged texting session. However, he was cooking and catching up on chores around the house. After answering the first few texts promptly, he became a little irregular in his responses. They had swapped names by this stage. It had also been agreed that they would meet on Tuesday at 11:40 a.m. in Coleraine Railway Station.

Some time later, he looked at his phone to find a message hinting that she wasn't happy about his failure to respond. He didn't understand. They had already made their arrangement. What more was there to discuss before they met?

By this time, they had shared a few pictures. He didn't find her particularly attractive. She was supposedly sixty-four, but she looked quite a bit older. He got to thinking. If she looked disagreeable in a picture, what would she look like in the flesh? There was a hint of a red flag somewhere, but he continued anyway.

As he lay in bed on Monday night, this imminent meeting played on his mind. He was without any sense of excitement or anticipation. There were no thoughts of romance, no fantasising, no reveries. But he had made a commitment. He had to go through with it now. Was it shaping up to be a first and last date all in one?

The following morning, he was up and away. Once settled on the train, he briefly scanned the news headlines. Nothing of importance. He put the phone away. He was struck by the fleet of buses parked up behind Antrim station. Had they nowhere to go? He took out a book and read intermittently for the rest of the journey. There was nothing of great interest along the way. No scenery to speak of, barring green fields, cowless, lifeless. He didn't even notice Ballymena. Cullybackey had one street lined with flags while another one was totally flagless. He surmised that there was a class divide in play. There was little thought about the upcoming tryst. He was in Coleraine before he knew it.

In Coleraine station, there was no immediate sign of his date. After visiting the bathroom, he had a walk around the concourse. Most of the recently arrived passengers had scattered. He looked into the coffee shop.

One lady sat alone at a table reading a book. He was sure it wasn't her.

Perhaps she was waiting outside. As he exited the station, she suddenly appeared right there in front of him. He looked at her, and she looked at him. She was a tall, slim woman. She carried herself well. Stylishly dressed but not a looker. Plain, to put it mildly. Even though she was plastered in makeup, he could see her skin was chapped and wrinkled. There was a brownish-pinky kind of sheen about her cheeks. The colour abruptly changed to normal just below the line of her jaw.

He knew in that moment that she wasn't for him.

She continued to look him up and down. Rugged but handsome in his own way. Jet black hair, brown eyes, and a dimple in his chin. But shorter than herself. She still had her doubts. Reservations were set aside as they greeted each other in a polite but lukewarm kind of way.

She paused before asking, "Where would you like to go?"

"Well, I'm a stranger here. Where would you suggest?"

"Coffee?"

"Great idea!"

"But not at my house!"

"I never mentioned your house."

"Joking! Let's go to The Railway Bar. It's just round the corner."

The Railway Bar was dark inside, yet the ambience was pleasant enough and the barmaid greeted them warmly. As he ordered the coffee, he was informed that they had no coffee machine. The girl was almost apologetic. There was only instant coffee. He turned to his date. She said it would do. While he waited for the drinks, she went off and took a seat by the window.

They sat down to two cups of tepid coffee.

"How was your journey?"

"Fine. Nothing too exciting, I must say."

"How long did it take?"

"About an hour and twenty."

"Thank you for coming. I suppose you're used to travelling around to meet ladies."

"Why do you say that?"

"Are you sure you're not married?"

He wasn't expecting this kind of onslaught and was a little slow in replying.

"No, I'm single."

"Are you divorced?"

"Not yet. It's complicated."

"I'm getting the impression you are a difficult person."

"Why?"

"Because you are evasive. And sometimes don't reply to my messages. Very like the actions of a man who is married or has someone in the background."

He was taken aback. To him, this was no big deal. He was sure she was reading too much into this.

"It's bad manners to ignore a text!"

"Am I expected to sit by the phone, ready to respond to messages instantly?"

"You knew I was waiting. You just decided not to reply."

"I live alone. Sometimes there are things that need doing. And I have never ignored you. I always reply as soon as possible."

"My circumstances are similar to yours, but I always reply to you promptly."

"So you're saying I should drop everything else when you're in texting mood?"

The chat turned to her work, her colleagues, and how much she enjoyed teaching.

"I started off in Derry. Later, I moved to Drogheda."

"What brought you to Coleraine?"

"I met a man from Coleraine, married him, and moved here."

"Have you any children?"

"No. I married in my fifties, and it was too late for children. How about you?"

"I have three daughters. They are all married. Are you separated or divorced?"

"I've been divorced for two years now."

"Me too. I've been single for a long time though. What happened?"

"My husband left me for another man. I stayed on here after he left."

"Was it as bad as a man leaving for another woman?"

"It was worse. You can't compete with a man. After he left, I devoted myself to my work. I teach two days a week and work one day as a personal stylist."

He didn't know what the latter job entailed. He thought it better not to ask.

She went on to talk about Rasharkin and her upbringing there. The pub she was reared in. Her father who was deceased. Her mother who had moved to Ballycastle when the father died.

"How do you find the dating scene?" he ventured.

"I am less than impressed. Men are all the same, obsessed with everything below the waist."

"How many men have you dated so far?"

"I'm relatively new to Tinder. In fact, I haven't had a proper date so far. I have met three men for coffee. One of them then decided to stalk me."

"Really! What happened?"

"He landed into my workplace. That's what happened."

"Why did you let him know where you worked?"

"I made the mistake of meeting him in a coffee shop next door to my office."

"It's different for men."

"I'm sure it is," she replied sarcastically.

"You don't believe me."

"Hmmm," she scoffed.

"OK, I'll give you an example. Some time back, I arranged to meet a lady just like today. She was set on going to a restaurant. Once there, she ordered starters, main course, dessert, wine, the lot. Everything was going swimmingly. The conversation flowed. However, as soon as we had polished it all off, her mood changed. She was stricken with a pain in her ankle. Soon it got so bad she had to leave. She assured me she would be in touch. I had to foot a hefty bill. Never heard of her again from that day to this."

She smiled and nodded her head but said nothing.

So he went on:

"I've made up my mind about first meetings. From now on, it's coffee. Coffee only. Like today. No more restaurants. Not on a first date."

She still didn't comment. Instead, she went on to speak of her own terms and conditions.

"I do have certain expectations. I think it's very important that people respect each other. I don't want to marry again. Nor do I want to live with anyone again. I would be open to a man visiting. Even staying overnight. But no one will be moving in."

Then she switched to religion.

"My faith means a lot to me. It is a big part of my life. When things look bleak, it always gets me through. I go to church every Sunday."

"I hate religion, in all its forms and manifestations."

There was a lengthy silence. Her face darkened. Finally, she looked him straight in the eye.

"In my opinion, we have nothing in common. I don't think this is going anywhere," she declared as she reached for her bag.

He paid the bill, £2 for the two coffees. Ironically, the cheapest coffee in a long time. They walked out together. Both dazed. Both speechless. It was only when she stopped to light a cigarette they realised they ought to be going their separate ways. She announced she had to go to the bank. He said he would go back to the station. They wished each other well. She headed one way and he headed the other.

He was just as she had suspected. A godless heathen. How could such a man have any principles? Not once did he give her a straight answer. Slippery as an eel. Probably a misogynist. Despite his protestations, she still couldn't be sure if he was single. To top it off, he had bad breath.

As he travelled homewards, he reflected on the lady, her life as described to him, her attitude to men, her certainties, and her judgemental nature. She expected others to fall in with her way of thinking, of doing things and conducting affairs, to coin a phrase. In mitigation, she'd had some traumatic experiences which must have coloured her outlook.

Even though it was now twilight, he could see the flags were still fluttering in Cullybackey. The fleet of buses still sat motionless in Antrim. And the green fields were still empty.

In the end, both had to accept that not many are lucky in love.

His hope was that the next one would be more beautiful.

Her hope was that the next one would be more forthcoming.

When the Music Died

Over the years, Peter had tried online dating from time to time, but without any great deal of success. He would try it for a few weeks. Sometimes he found it exhausting. He was coming off a prolonged break when he decided to give it another go.

Initially, he matched with several ladies. He was particularly drawn to Carole. She always responded promptly. From the beginning, Peter sensed that it was her first venture into internet dating. He could tell by her openness at times and by her uncertainty at other times.

They exchanged all the usual information—personal details, work, and locations. A musician, she lived in Wexford. He was a project manager in Galway for a construction company.

"I know distances can be overcome and all that, but... I'll need convincing," she wrote with a hint of doubt.

"We can write anyway!" he suggested hopefully.

"I work four days a week plus five nights till 8:00 p.m. I sometimes play on weekends. My instruments are the harp and violin. My children, 13 and 10, are still at home, and I only have every other weekend off."

"That sounds like a busy schedule!"

"Can you imagine how I would not want to drive to Galway for a coffee?"

Peter had posted a few pictures on his profile, one a younger him with a full head of long, flowing hair and a beard.

"Explain what a man would need hair extensions for?" she quipped. "Did you play the main part in a passion play?"

"I was a student," he replied, a touch defensively. "It was common to have long hair at that time."

Carole was always busy. "You'll have to forgive me. I can't log on every night."

"If we are to meet, I'll have to go to Wexford?" he ventured.

"Do you have a helicopter? Call me Carole, by the way."

"I'm Peter."

"Still thinking of that picture of you with the long thick hair. My hair is nearly down to my waist—but you might still outshine me!"

"I wouldn't worry too much about it. Mine is much shorter and thinner these days."

"Did you try to send me your phone number?" she asked. "Numbers get deleted unless you're a premium member."

"I should have known," Peter replied.

"I'm not a premium member either. They'll get their money's worth when I upgrade. If you've waited this long for Mrs Right, you can wait a bit longer. I'll keep writing and, when I get time, I might even upload a picture."

"I'm sure you're beautiful!" Peter wrote.

"Don't worry. Even 14-year-olds look at me. I feel like telling them I could be their mum. But my lads keep my feet on the ground. They tell me I'm fat and ugly!"

"Last remark before logging off. You don't sound like a man who works in construction!"

"Well, I am. And I'm tone-deaf!" Peter retorted good-naturedly.

"How would tone-deaf fit in with a musician?" Carole exclaimed. "It's getting late. Stay in touch. After only a few days on this, I keep thinking that if I don't find romance, I'll find friends!"

From experience, Peter was doubtful about finding friends in this environment but didn't comment.

Peter was quite happy to let Carole take the lead. He had been through the whole process before. Better to go with the flow. She was endlessly inquisitive. He was quite happy answering random lists of questions. Their exchanges became more intense, more personal.

They discussed their pasts, their families, the winding roads that had led them to this digital intersection.

"How long were you married, Peter?"

"Twenty years."

"Same here. How old were you when you got married?"

"Thirty."

"Obviously a late calling to fatherhood! And obviously not with Mrs Right? I married young; I was only twenty. I assume your kids live with their mother?"

"Yes. I have three daughters and a son."

"Kids are wonderful, and I hope you stay in touch with them!"

"Yes, I see them nearly every day."

"My boys see their dad once a fortnight at the weekend. I wish he'd do some more during the week."

"From your profile, it sounds like you do plenty of travelling. Can you explain what it is that makes you want to do that?" she queried.

"It's a good way to escape when things get too much."

She kept coming back to his profile picture.

"Please explain the Jesus look? Do you want to attract stoned hippies? Can't you upload something recent?"

"I've already taken it down and replaced it. Happy now?"

"I've been trying to scan and upload a picture but without any luck so far."

"I'm still in the dark. But I have no doubt that you're absolutely gorgeous."

"Thank you. I might not be your type at all, but if there's no chemistry, we can have fun writing. I'll finish tonight with a quote by Oscar Wilde: Bigamy is having one wife too many. Monogamy is the same."

"What if you have no wife?" he thought to himself.

There was always a new topic to discuss. She was endlessly curious.

"Forgot to ask: last book you read and book you are reading now, if any. Also your birthday. I am reading *Star of the Sea* by Joe O'Connor. Will go to bed soon and read a bit more."

"I'm reading *The Wind-Up Bird Chronicle*. I have read *Star of the Sea*." He gave her his date of birth in longhand—numbers would be deleted.

"In the meantime, tell me more. Can you laugh at Woody Allen? What's your fav alcoholic drink? What's your ideal holiday look like? What do you like to achieve still? Are you a communicator? Which reminds me, do you like music? … classical? Have you ever been to an opera?"

This was all a lot to take in at once for Peter. He tried his best to reply.

"I sometimes laugh at Woody but not always. My favourite drink is Guinness. I like to travel to countries where they don't speak English. Adds a sense of adventure. As regards aims, goals, and targets, I need to think more about those. Can't you see I am a communicator? I used to be very much into rock music. Not so much these days."

When in doubt, she always came back to his profile.

"How did you write that profile? How did you choose what to put in?"

"I just included what I thought a lady might want to know."

"Like this? — 'Looking for someone to join me on spontaneous adventures.' That could mean anything."

"That was what came to mind at the time. Spontaneous, to coin a word!"

"Actually, I do like it. Spontaneity is rare. Generally, people want candlelit dinners, walks on the beach, a GSOH, a partner in crime. They like music and food. Tells you nothing."

"I enjoy writing to you and find myself looking forward to it," Peter wrote, surprised at what he'd admitted.

"Me too. I enjoy writing, but I also enjoy talking. I like a good debate. But... I did make the mistake of not allowing myself enough time before. I was barely twenty when I hooked up with my ex, and I intend to make sure that this time I'm totally comfortable before hooking up again."

"That is understandable, but there are so many variables. It's hard to know where to start sometimes. However, you will know very quickly if you really like someone," Peter replied.

"The converse is also true!" she cautioned.

They talked about chemistry, about intuition, about how some people just clicked. They shared small things: Carole's morning routine, her teaching day, running errands, cooking, even repairing lawnmowers, practising for her own pleasure. Peter wrote about his daughters, about reading *One Hundred Years of Solitude*, and the fun of their correspondence.

He found her fascinating—intense in the best way. A mind in motion. She was funny too, with a nose so sensitive she could smell when her kids were about to get sick.

"So don't be afraid, Peter. You can still run before I become a premium member!"

He laughed out loud reading that and replied, "Too late. I've upgraded. Besides, Carole, I want to hear your voice one of these days, not to mention your music."

One day Peter announced, "I'm going to Mayo tomorrow. I'm to attend a Black Tie event over the weekend."

"Oh. Enjoy! What's it in aid of?"

"The local football club."

"As to sports—I'm lost. Know nothing of any sports. Had a sports bypass. As to black tie events, I played at loads of them. Can be fun if you're in good company. You might bump into Mrs Right."

"You never know, lol!"

"Just uploaded a picture and access for you. If it doesn't work, let me know. What a pity you are gone because during the weekend there's more time for writing. Will you upload a more recent photograph? I did not get your date of birth, so please resend. Mine's the fourteenth of this month. I do ask lots and have been told I'm demanding."

"It wasn't me that said that," Peter replied playfully.

"Even my car mechanic says it! At the moment, thoroughly enjoying the writing—and the fact that you are open for that is great."

"I must be doing something right."

"I found myself looking forward to going online tonight. I will hold my horses till we meet because there are so many aspects to a person. The way somebody walks, moves, curls a lip, laughs. Another question: do you laugh ha ha ha sounds or eh eh eh sounds? Just recently analysing my twenty years of marriage. In all that time, he never once laughed an open laugh, if you know what I mean."

He went off to Ballina on Friday. When he arrived, he typed off a quick message.

"Just arrived in Mayo. Mother had dinner waiting. About to get ready for the event. Keep well. Talk soon."

Her inquisitiveness continued, touching on everything from his mother to his habits.

"Saw that you somehow logged on this evening. Your ma's laptop, no doubt. My mum has one now and she goes online to play cards."

Later again… "Looked at your profile and saw that you smoke occasionally. What does that mean? You can live without it? One a day? At parties only? Oh, and if you wonder if I'm inquisitive, the answer is yes. I just feel I need to communicate to get to know someone."

"Yes, my mother's a force of nature. As for smoking, it's really just occasional—nothing I couldn't cut out entirely. Glad to hear of your concern."

He asked if she would soon be a premium member so they could share phone numbers.

"I'll be a premium member when I want to. Fate has it that I might have to travel up to Limerick next weekend to look at a second-hand harp. Nearer the time I'll find out if that would suit you. If so, I'll sign up for full membership to enable us to make arrangements."

Peter replied, sharing some thoughts of his own. "I believe there is such a thing as chemistry. We can't know whether we have it or not until we meet. I also believe that some people connect much easier than others. They have some kind of universal connection. Others only rarely connect no matter how hard they try. But we have to be positive."

She replied, "Can there be such a thing as digital chemistry? If that could only come across face to face too? I received pictures of the harp. Looks wonderful. I'll definitely go and look at it. Whatever, I will sign up during the week. You should be able to see my private picture. Can't see any phone number. Was it deleted?"

Peter replied, "Hi Carole, you're right, that message probably had my number in it. The site's security measures are a bit annoying, aren't they?"

"Finally got to see your picture. Very vague, but I like the hair better than the Nazareth style. Prefer the clean-shaven too! For me it will be about how you talk, move, laugh, etc. And call me weird, but smell is important too. Now don't overdose on aftershave! I mean the actual unique personal smell that everybody has."

"Thank you. But I still haven't seen your picture! No worries though."

When he had returned to Galway, they began to plan for their first live, face-to-face encounter.

"Looking forward to our first meeting. If we click, great. If not, we save ourselves a lot of driving. You must have written and even met people before."

Peter replied, "Yes, I've met people online before. No one of consequence though. Can you be the one? I like how you write. Can't wait to meet now."

"I'm not nervous. This feels right somehow. Strange how you can 'know' someone without meeting. The spark—well, we'll see."

"I've always believed in instinct. Let's see what transpires," he answered confidently.

"Good! Because mine told me to write back to you."

"I'm impressed. A harpist, a fixer, a parent, a teacher… and a great correspondent. I'm curious—do you ever get time to sleep?" he asked.

She came back with, "Rarely! But I try. As for you—green tea drinker and gives hugs? Good. But if we hit it off, that scares me too. The distance! We're both tied to family and work."

"Let's keep things simple. Coffee, a walk, a chat. That's all we need to start."

She agreed. "I just need good company. Someone outgoing. So many people bottle things up. You seem to speak your mind. I'll leave the venue to you—but keep it easy to reach. I don't need scenery to get to know you! I'll be coming in on the N18."

"I've had a look at the map. How about The Old Ground Hotel in Ennis? It's just off the N18, and it's a good halfway point. Perfect for a chat and maybe some lunch. I'll text you details later today. Don't worry about the photo. I'll see you in person anyway!"

"Perfect. I subscribed just for the month—never thought I'd have to pay to get someone's number! Shows how I feel. I like your thoughts on happiness, too. Why are some people content with little, others miserable with much? I think staying curious and connected is the key."

"I feel the same. I'd rather have a glass of wine and a good talk than a night out drinking just for the sake of it."

"Exactly. That said, maybe once in a while I'd like to whoop it up in a club! Looking forward to tomorrow. Don't know what to wear yet, but I'll figure it out. I do tend to wear skirts. See you soon, Peter."

"Likewise. Whatever happens, I've really enjoyed it so far."

The night before the meeting, their messages crackled with anticipation. Carole was very excited.

"Thinking about tomorrow. Tomorrow will tell if my instincts function well over the airwaves or if they are useless. It is the very first time I meet somebody this way. Looking forward to a mixture of madness and sanity, fun and seriousness. Somebody who is like me but not too much so. Will take another look at your picture."

Then she followed up, "You know the way, when you don't know somebody and there might be just that little bit of doubt. Did she really send it? Is she like the lady with the beard? Does she look ten years older? A real hag?"

She confirmed her photo issues were genuine, a glitch beyond her control.

Peter was a little more cautious. He had been here before and tried to keep it low-key. "I know it's easy to say, but behave as you would in any other meeting. Be relaxed. And you should know by now that I'm very easy-going."

Saturday arrived. Carole, having settled the harp business, drove to Ennis. In The Old Ground, Peter was already waiting, nervous but hopeful. He rose as she approached, a pleasant smile on his face. They exchanged polite greetings, a little awkwardness in the air—a stark contrast to the easy flow of their written words. To Peter, Carole seemed ultra tense, distant, unused to this game, a rabbit in the headlights.

They found a quiet table. Carole, always observant, paid careful attention as he spoke. He talked about his work, his kids, his travels—reiterating much of what he'd already written. She found him to be much as she expected: a steady-as-you-go type of man. He listened when she spoke, and his responses were thoughtful.

Yet, as they talked, Carole felt nothing. The "digital chemistry" she'd felt so strongly—the online spark—didn't translate into the real world. His laugh didn't quite resonate. His presence didn't stir any deep feeling. She realised that while he was a good man, interesting, and kind – he wasn't her man. The pull just wasn't there.

As they parted ways, polite smiles still on their faces, both knew that they would not meet again. Carole felt no real connection. Peter was strongly aware of a coolness that had set in the moment they met.

The next day, Peter received an email from Carole. Before he even read it, he knew what was in it.

"I needed some time to myself before writing to you. I've been up a while but I'm still in my dressing gown. Thank you for coming up to see me yesterday. What can I say about it? You seemed familiar and yet strange.

You seem a very nice man. I know you possess qualities I would be looking for, but I don't think I have met the man I am dreaming of. I don't know exactly what he is like, but I have a mental test. I ask myself: 'Is this the man I want to walk along the beach with, holding hands?'

I hope you find the woman of your dreams and I wish you all the best.

I enjoyed writing to you.

PS: Just reread some of your emails and actually did enjoy the writing. As you wrote, there are many imponderables, and whether the right chemistry is there is something we cannot control."

Peter reread the email, then deleted it. Nothing left but a bittersweet taste in his mouth. He sighed, reflecting on yet another familiar experience in the brutal world of online dating: when the written word clashes with reality— the hopeful buildup, the fleeting euphoria, the sudden deflation.

He didn't even think of replying. What was the point?

Just disengage totally and think of new possibilities.

The Wrong Gerri

Tony had just recently returned to Ireland after spending seven years teaching English in Japan. He had left in a hurry. A job offer out of the blue. So good he couldn't turn it down. Now, back on Irish soil, he was sifting through old diaries, attempting to reconnect with the life he'd left behind.

He eventually discovered the phone numbers of several old friends, even some old flames. Among those was a number for Gerri, a lady he had often thought of during those years away.

"Would she even remember me?"

"Would she want to see me after all this time?"

"Was she still in the country?"

"Maybe married now!"

He didn't attempt contact for a couple of weeks while he thought it over.

Finally, almost inevitably, he couldn't resist writing.

The message was simple: "Hello, how are you, Gerri?" Bland but safe.

Her reply was swift. "Hi, who's asking? And thank you… Good."

He stared at his phone. The reply was cold, wary. No recognition. Seven years was a long time. He was now a stranger.

"This is Tony. I lost your number in 2016. Glad you're well."

"Hope all's good with you too… Jeepers. And may I ask, where have you been in the meantime?"

"I was in Japan."

"Wow, that sounds interesting. Why Japan?"

"I was teaching over there."

"Tony, how do you know me?"

He tried to jolt her memory by pulling details from his past with his Gerri.

"Remember we met a few times! I visited you once and we met in Oranmore a few times. You were living in Peter Ryan's house."

"OK. I've no idea. I have a feeling you're mixing me up."

He persisted, recalling more specifics:

"Oh, you told me stories about the nuns when you first came to Ireland. Your son played rugby."

Her responses grew more baffling.

"Ok, now I've got you! You got back with your wife. Bumped into you and your wife a few times at Jazz sessions too. I was beginning to think this was a scam! I've always had my own house! With Covid etc no Jazz yet… Hopefully, by spring it will be back."

Mystified, he replied, "No, that's not me."

"Oh, did you cook me dinner? You had an apartment in Oranmore?" she ventured hopefully.

His heart dropped. There was definitely something amiss.

"You also told me about your car accident at the Terryland roundabout. We talked about your visit to

225

Tangles Hair Salon in Ardrahan to get your hair done. You went with a friend and you had vouchers but the owner refused to honour them. I remember because I knew the husband. I lived in Athenry then."

"Ah, you've lost me... No accident... Never get hair done... Where did you get my number?"

"I found it in an old diary."

"Phone me!"

He didn't phone immediately. Their online exchange had only muddied the waters, leaving him with a sense of déjà vu, or perhaps, deja non-vu. He needed to get things straight in his head first. He checked the diary. The phone number was okay. Just that her memories didn't match his at all. His mind drifted back, seven years disappearing in an instant. He recalled their last meeting with vivid clarity, as if it were just yesterday. They had arranged in advance for him to go to her house. She would make dinner. She was to wait for him in a hotel car park near her house.

He could still hear the rain beating off the windscreen as he pulled into that car park. He was late. When he called, she had answered immediately.

"Finally!" she answered, her voice sharp but amused. "I was beginning to think you'd forgotten about me."

"Traffic," he sighed. "And a phone call that wouldn't end."

"Look to your left."

Indeed there she was, sheltering under a big multicoloured umbrella.

Gerri had warned Tony about her house—a "miner's cottage," she called it, with broken windows, doors hanging off their hinges and a leaky roof. She said she had done a bit of work on it. The landlord had promised to do a lot of things for her and hadn't done any. She pointed to a crack in the doorstep.

As she led him inside, he was surprised. It seemed in good shape and very homely. A lot of work had been done on it. At a glance it appeared that the windows all seemed to be functioning. Likewise the doors. Floors had been tiled, walls painted, the stairs moved, furniture bought and a kitchen fitted. Even the back garden, dotted with children's toys, was neatly kept.

"I thought you said this place was a wreck."

"Oh, it was," she replied, filling the kettle. "But I've put twenty grand into it. The landlord promised to help—Jim Sheridan, a friend of my son's. Useless." She rolled her eyes. "I was going to buy it, but now? Not a chance."

He glanced around. "You've done well. It's… cosy."

She smirked. "Cosy. That's one word for it," she countered as she aimed a kick at a poorly hung door.

The dinner itself was hardly memorable. She wasn't a great cook, but she could talk for Ireland. She recounted some recent incidents—two car accidents, one where her vehicle flipped, another where it caught fire. She had had a narrow escape.

"Two men rescued me," she said, tapping her spine. "But they had to do it so quickly. I twisted my back as they pulled me out. Then afterwards the insurance company refused to pay out. Usual story. Some technicality."

She turned the spotlight on Tony. "Now, your turn. Japan? The women? Tell me everything."

He laughed. "Women! One wanted to marry me. A few others hinted at it."

"And did you?"

"No, not yet," he deflected.

And of course she had to ask him a question to put him on the spot, "What do you want?"

"At this stage just dessert," he jested.

They both laughed.

The conversation turned darker when she spoke of her early days in Ireland. She was part of a team of psychiatric nurses who had been recruited in England. They were assigned to various mental institutions run by various religious orders. She was posted to Ballinasloe.

"They used us as guinea pigs," she said bitterly. "The government wanted to know what was really happening behind those walls."

She described walking in on a naked man standing in a basin of water while a nun stood by. "No towel, nothing. I kicked up a racket. The nun threatened to have me fired."

Then came the bombshell. "I told them I had a direct line to the Vatican."

"You what?" Tony nearly choked on his tea.

She grinned. "A relative was a deacon there. I showed them the proof. The head brother panicked. Next thing? The nun vanished. The brother hanged himself. They blocked up the room where he did it—like it never existed."

He could never forget Gerri regaling him with a series of fantastic stories, one after the other. The murder of the woman in Tuam had a strong hint of mystery and many unresolved issues. In that case the husband served several years in jail. But there was more to it. An affair with a married policeman, a baby on the way and the cop being blackmailed.

Then the story of the hairdresser in Ardrahan whose special offer wasn't really so special at all. Gerri had to pay the full amount. The husband of the hairdresser, a farmer, known as a chancer too. Gerri had heard of him selling sick beasts that died soon afterwards.

Gerri had talked of family matters. First up had been her ex-husband, Mervyn, who was now deceased. The man was from the north. When he died he had been owed a lot of money. He had been very generous, lending out money to people he would meet in bars and other places of entertainment.

"One guy owes me 22 million euros but I don't know where he is or even what he looks like."

Tony nearly choked again.

"Others owe lesser amounts. I have given up hope of recovering anything."

Then there was her ex-husband's grandson. Mervyn had been married before and this was a problem child.

"I remember once I was up in Belfast. The boy was sixteen at the time. He locked himself in a room when he was high on drugs. The police were called. They broke down the door and found bags of drugs and large sums of money."

Gerri had a cousin Tom who seemed to act as friend, adviser and frequent visitor.

There was a story about dinosaur eggs and a bucket of water. Tony couldn't really follow it. Tom had to come and break out the dinosaurs with a hammer when the kids weren't looking, but they were so ugly. The kids went on holiday. They were looking for dinosaur babies when they came back. Ber replaced them with two nicer dinos. There had also been something about 2 robins but at that point Tony's memory ran out.

He'd laughed then, unsure how much to believe. Now, replaying the bizarre recollections, he wondered—had any of it been real? This comedy of errors, wrong memories, mistaken identities, tumbled through his mind. It just didn't make sense. Snapping back to the present, the phone felt heavy in his hand. For better or worse, he decided to make the call.

When he finally made the call, the voice on the other end was unmistakably not Gerri's. This Gerri was Irish, her soft tone a stark contrast to the sharp, Liverpool cadence he remembered. The confusion only deepened.

"You've got the wrong woman," the lady said, amused.

But she laughed like she'd been waiting. "So, tell me about Japan."

"Well, I was there for seven years. Great experience. Made many friends. Sadly now it's all over. They refused to renew my contract."

"And here I was thinking of that man in Oranmore who made me dinner. Unforgettable evening. It was so romantic. Sitting there watching the sun go down on Galway Bay. And now it appears it wasn't you at all!!"

"I don't think so. If it had been me I would surely remember."

"Do you play golf?"

"Not really, no."

"I play twice a week. I love it. I've been a member at Barna Golf Club for years."

She paused, then out of the blue, "I know this is mad but maybe we should meet up."

Two days before Christmas Tony went to meet Gerri at the Huntsman, a pub in the shadow of the Connacht Rugby stadium. It was 10:30 in the morning. The place was busy. It took a while to find her. She was sitting away at the back, coffee in hand and smiling broadly as he approached. They shook hands and Tony went off to order a drink. She looked about his own age but very different from the Gerri he knew. As soon as he had sat down she launched into her story…

"I used to live in Barna. I then moved to Knocknacarra and lived on the main road which strangely was very private. I did know my next door neighbours though. They were very nice."

"I know Barna. I have some friends over that way."

"After my divorce I did a lot of business courses and ran a few businesses. I used to have a kennels and kept dogs for holidaymakers."

No end to this woman's talents, Tony thought— golfer, businesswoman, dog sitter.

"And you are single?" he queried.

"Yes, at the minute." She laughed before going on.

"I divorced about 20 years ago but was in a relationship for some time afterwards. I then had a brief liaison with a man whom I had known a long time. He turned out to be very narcissistic, self-centred, always looking for approval and praising himself."

"How did you handle that, Gerri?"

"I finished it. Thankfully, because of Covid, I haven't run into him since."

"Look at this." Gerri invited Tony to look at her bruised ankle. "I was playing football a few days ago."

"You play football?" asked a startled Tony.

"Well, I'm a country girl at heart. I don't need many material things to make me happy. Mind you, I spent a few years working in Dublin too."

"You get around!" exclaimed Tony.

"I guess I do."

"What's your plan for today?"

"Actually I'm en route to Kinvara to see my daughter and the grandchildren."

She showed him photos of the grandchildren.

"You'd like Kinvara," she said. "Quiet. Unspoiled. Beautiful views. Great pubs."

Gerri looked at her watch. "Anyway, I gotta go. Doesn't time fly when you're having fun?"

He almost asked about the Vatican but caught himself in time. He nodded. "We should meet again."

She smiled. "Next time you're around."

Later, he wondered about the real Gerri—where she'd gone, if she was still at war with the landlord and the nuns.

Or had she, too, slipped into another life?

Had he ever known her at all?

Dressed to Deceive

Bernie was in her late forties but still retained the looks and figure that had turned heads in her younger days. Now two years a widow, she felt that the grieving process had run its course. She was still young, and it was time to move on. Recently, she had been discussing it with her sister Tess.

"You need something to occupy you, Bernie. Why don't you try Tinder?"

"I hadn't thought of that."

"It might be fun. Meet some interesting people. At the very least, it'll give you some kind of life outside the house."

Bernie was initially hesitant.

"I know it is a new opportunity, but on the other hand, there could be pitfalls. The fear of the unknown, I suppose."

"Don't worry. I'll be here for you if you're in doubt about anything."

She had been warned that once you entered this arena, you had to be prepared for scammers, hackers, liars and stalkers. Many people misrepresented themselves. Tess tried to reassure her.

"All things considered, I think the positives outweigh the negatives. For mature adults, making new connections isn't easy."

Bernie decided to sleep on it. The next day when they met, she was feeling more confident about it.

"OK Tess. I suppose nothing ventured, nothing gained. I'll give it a go. If it doesn't work for me, I can always quit."

"I'm glad to hear that. Remember, you will be able to control who you meet up with. There is safety in getting to know people a little before meeting. And you have always been careful."

Tess helped Bernie create a profile. In her bio she provided all the standard personal details and a personal statement.

@freebird: "Adventurous, kind, and always up for a good laugh!"

"Hi there! I'm a young-at-heart, empathetic, independent woman who enjoys life's little pleasures. Whether it's trying out a new recipe, a weekend away or going to a concert, I believe in making the most of every moment. I'm passionate about health, good coffee, and meaningful conversations. I consider myself a good listener and value honesty, kindness, and a good sense of humour. If you can make me laugh, we're already off to a great start! Looking for someone who's genuine, spontaneous, and ready to share life's ups and downs. Let's see where this journey takes us!"

Almost immediately, Bernie began to get attention. Sometimes it was full-on attention. Even though she approached it with her eyes open, she was still taken aback by the directness, impatience and, at times, rudeness of the men. If you weren't up for meeting immediately, they just moved on. They didn't seem to want to get to know her.

They wanted women who were available right now to meet, and more.

For a time, she didn't know what to say or do. She often felt like giving up. So much wasted energy. This online dating was turning out to be a test of patience and emotional endurance. While it was exciting at times, it was equally frustrating, tiring and, at times, bewildering. She enjoyed chatting to some of the people, but she didn't want to rush into anything. Even though she was determined to move on, she was still readjusting to the sudden death of her husband. Tess, of course, was always in the background urging her to be cautious while she familiarised herself with the nuances of online dating.

Through time, she began to gain confidence. She began to recognise the various types of characters. Their profile pictures often revealed a lot. Men with pictures of tractors or lawnmowers were an instant turn-off, as were dog dads and rugby dads. She wasn't able to keep up with the fitness fanatics or the skydivers, fishermen or hikers. Some were obsessed with things like food, travel, reading or poetry. She found that few listened and many talked incessantly about themselves and their pastimes. Others wanted to vent, usually about previous partners.

Bernie was always friendly but kept a distance. For some time, she avoided getting to the point of phoning or meeting anyone. Then came Dessie, the lawyer from Dublin. He hit a nerve with Bernie. He didn't talk a lot about himself. This was the first person who asked about her and listened to what she had to say. He had a dry, self-deprecating sense of humour that she found refreshing. She felt comfortable with him. From his picture, he certainly looked handsome.

In terms of build, Dessie appeared to be tall and athletic, with a powerful frame that spoke of an active lifestyle. She later found out he had played rugby in his youth. His dark, wavy hair, strong jawline, and mischievous twinkle in his blue eyes gave him a rugged yet refined look. Bernie felt an instant connection.

It wasn't long until they arranged to meet. Their first date was set for a hotel in Athlone, not far from Bernie's home in Roscommon. When Bernie arrived there, there wasn't a sinner in sight apart from the two ladies on reception. After visiting the restroom and freshening up, she called Dessie. He assured her he was nearby. She wandered around the lobby looking at various posters and notices. Dessie breezed in a few minutes later and, without hesitation, greeted Bernie with a warm hug and presented her with a big bunch of roses.

Clearly, Dessie was both striking and charismatic. He had perfectly gelled hair and a fair complexion. His smile was infectious, with a hint of playfulness. With his tweed jacket, crisp white shirt, dark jeans and well-polished shoes, he exuded an air of sophistication.

They sat down at the nearest table and Dessie ordered drinks. It was a quiet time in the hotel. Two middle-aged men sat at the bar watching snooker. Three ladies sat nearby with their coats on and bags on their laps.

Three more then joined them, whereupon the whole flock headed out on the town.

When they had made themselves comfortable, Dessie began to tell Bernie about a strange character he had met outside. Bernie laughed.

"I know him!"

"You mean the bearded dwarf on crutches?"

"Yes, he is a regular here. He comes every weekend."

"Well, he was leaning against the wall out there, smoking what looked like a spliff!"

"Sounds about right for Oliver. You'd never guess he has a high-level job in the civil service."

"Really?"

"There's sometimes more to people than meets the eye. He once tried it on with me but let's not go there."

The conversation flowed, as if they had known each other for years rather than just through their two weeks of online messages. Dessie's easygoing nature and quick wit kept Bernie laughing. She found herself relaxing more than she had in a long time. The initial awkwardness of meeting someone new, especially in the context of online dating, melted away as they shared stories about their lives, their families, good times and bad times.

As the evening wore on, the conversation shifted to more personal topics. Dessie opened up about his divorce a few years earlier. It had taken him a while before he felt ready to date again. Bernie found herself sharing more about her late husband, Michael, and how his sudden passing had left her feeling adrift for so long. It was strange, she thought, how comfortable she felt talking to Dessie about things she hadn't even fully processed herself.

At one point, Dessie reached across the table and gently placed his hand over hers.

"You've been through a lot, Bernie," he said softly. "But you've got amazing strength and determination. I can see it."

Bernie felt a lump form in her throat.

"Thank you," she whispered.

As the night drew to a close, Dessie walked Bernie to her car.

"I had a great time tonight," he said, his voice sincere. "I'd love to see you again, if you're up for it."

Bernie smiled, feeling a flutter of nervous excitement.

"I'd like that," she said. "I really would."

Dessie leaned in and kissed her cheek, his stubble brushing against her skin.

"Take care, Bernie. I'll call you soon."

As she drove home, Bernie couldn't stop smiling. She was on cloud nine. For the first time in a long time, she felt there was a future. Maybe, just maybe, this was the start of something new. She couldn't wait to tell her sister Tess all about her evening.

Tess was waiting. Bernie had a feeling her sister might be a little jealous.

"How did the date go?"

"It was great. He exceeded all expectations!"

"Will you meet him again?"

"Yes. Maybe next weekend!"

"Just be careful. It takes time to fully get to know people. And you have had no experience of dating for years. Some of these guys can sniff out vulnerable women."

"I am aware of that, Tess."

The next weekend Bernie met Dessie again. This time they went for dinner. Once more, Dessie came across as a complete gentleman – so dapper, so suave. He paid for everything. Bernie was in dreamland. At the end of the evening, he again escorted Bernie to her car and this time kissed her on the lips.

For the third date, Bernie asked Dessie if he would like to come to her house. He agreed. As soon as he arrived, she put on the kettle. She even put two teabags in his cup. The tea was very strong but, in mitigation, it did come with cheese, tomatoes, smoked salmon and brown bread. While they were having tea, Bernie brought out a large selection of photographs of family and friends.

Dessie was charming, attentive, and always impeccably dressed. But there were moments that gave Bernie pause. His humour sometimes took a dark turn. She laughed nervously, unsure whether to be amused or concerned. His jokes were clever, but there was an undercurrent of something unsettling, a fascination with the absurd and the macabre. At one point, he leaned in close, his voice dropping to a whisper.

"Did you ever notice how quiet it gets just before something bad happens?"

She laughed, but later wondered, "Why did he say that?"

Tess then dropped in. She lived in the same estate. While Bernie was a petite blonde, Tess was tall and dark-haired, a few years younger than Bernie. Although Bernie sometimes referred to her sister as Mother Hen, they were very close. Tess had been her chief support when her husband died.

Just after Tess arrived, Bernie received a phone call and went off into another room. After a few minutes, she reappeared. She apologised but stated that she had to take the call. Dessie was very keen to know who Bernie had been talking to. Bernie passed it off. "Just a friend." He then said he'd better get going. It was late.

Bernie found herself both captivated and slightly unnerved. Dessie's eccentricity was undeniably magnetic, but there was a lingering sense that his humour was sometimes darker.

She passed it off as Dessie teasing her.

"Isn't he sweet, Tess?"

"Yes, Bernie. He is certainly handsome and very dapper. Just be careful! He seemed overly interested in who called you. That might not be healthy!"

Dessie became a regular weekend visitor. He showered Bernie with flowers and chocolates. His profession lent him an air of respectability, making Bernie less likely to question his intentions. On Saturday afternoons, he liked to watch football on TV. Bernie sensed he didn't like to be disturbed during games. It suited her. She would go off shopping for the duration.

One afternoon, Tess was helping Bernie with laundry when she noticed something strange. Bernie's favourite silk underwear was missing.

"Did you lose your silk undies?" Tess asked.

Bernie shrugged. "Oh, I must have misplaced them. No big deal."

"And when did you start colour-coding your dresses?"

"Oh stop being ridiculous, Tess. You're starting to annoy me."

But Tess wasn't convinced. She started paying closer attention and noticed that other items of Bernie's lingerie had gone missing over the weeks – a lace bra here, a satin camisole there. Bernie brushed it off as forgetfulness, but Tess's suspicions grew.

One Saturday afternoon, Tess arrived unannounced at Bernie's house. She let herself in with the spare key. Dessie was alone in the living room, watching TV. He seemed startled by her arrival but quickly recovered, flashing his charming smile.

"Tess! What a surprise. Bernie's just popped out to the shops."

Tess nodded, her eyes narrowing as she got a glimpse of black lace partially hidden under a cushion. She didn't say anything, but her mind was racing. At half-time, when Dessie left the room to make tea, she quickly lifted the cushion and found one of Bernie's bras underneath.

What the hell is he doing with her underwear? Tess wondered, her stomach churning. While Bernie was out, it appeared that Dessie wasn't just watching football.

When Dessie had gone home, Tess mentioned what she had seen on Saturday afternoon.

"Dessie's been going through your things," she said. "I found your bra under the cushion. And your wardrobe, it's like he's been rearranging your clothes."

Bernie hesitated. She still had this lingering thought that Tess was being jealous. Dessie's odd behaviour hadn't gone unnoticed, but she hadn't wanted to believe the worst. She had become used to his strange sense of humour and brushed it off as an idiosyncrasy, perhaps even a misguided attempt at being playful. No one was perfect.

When he was back home in Dublin, Dessie called Bernie every day. She welcomed this newfound attention. It showed that he cared. However, as time wore on, the calls became more frequent. At times, she felt they were a little intrusive. He always wanted to know where she was, who she was with, and what she was doing. Just another side to his personality?

While Bernie always made allowances for Dessie, Tess was more concerned about his odd habits. She could see a pattern emerging. Bernie had let slip that when he arrived at the weekend, he immediately headed to her bedroom, supposedly to drop his bag. But it was always quite a while before he came back downstairs. She went up once to check if he was OK and found him rummaging through her clothes. He said he was searching for a cufflink he had left behind last time.

Tess thought back to the argument over whether Bernie was colour-coding her clothes. Now she realised it must have been Dessie. She figured that he was arranging Bernie's clothes before he left on Sunday evening. That way, when he returned, he could go to her wardrobe to check which items had been worn during his absence. He could gauge how many times she had been out and whether this tallied with what he had been told. Tess didn't want to alarm her sister at this stage, so she kept her thoughts to herself.

Meanwhile, Bernie had come to accept that Dessie was sneaking into her room and messing with her clothes. She could see the signs that he had been there. As time went on, his actions grew more intrusive and unsettling. She wondered if she should pay more heed to Tess. It now appeared that he was doing more than just playing around with her clothes. Was he dressing up in her underwear? Even the thought of it made her skin creep. She must tell her sister, even though Tess was sure to say, "I told you so."

"You know I never took to that lad, right from that first night he arrived. Remember when he questioned you at length about that phone call?" said Tess.

"I forgot about that!"

"He has always struck me as a slippery character. Far too smooth. Too sweet to be wholesome. There's a bad eye in his head. When he makes eye contact, he seems to stare."

"What should I do? It really has gone too far now."

"Can we have a good look in your wardrobe?"

"Yes, why not!"

Tess was much more worldly than Bernie. Even though she had never been married, she had had several relationships – not all of them wonderful. She had knowledge of characters like Dessie. She recognised his behaviour. It wasn't just odd, it was controlling, invasive, and deeply unnerving. Probably narcissistic. A love bomber.

Tess looked in the wardrobe and then began to look around the bedroom.

"Where did you get that stuffed tiger? I never saw it before."

"Dessie bought it for me."

"Hmmm. Can I have a look at it?"

Tess started to examine the toy. She knew what she was looking for. Before long, she found a hidden camera built into it.

"Just as I suspected. Not only has he been messing around with your clothes, but I bet he's been taking pictures of you when you're undressed."

"Do you think so?"

"Yes. I think we also need to look in the bathroom. If he has put a camera here, there is a good chance there is one in there too."

They worked their way around the bathroom. Tess knew to look in vents and around plants and mirrors. However, after a few minutes, nothing had been found.

"Maybe there's only the one, Tess?"

"No, there's one here. I'm sure of it. Be patient. Can you bring me a chair?"

"What for?"

"I need it to stand on. I want to look in the smoke detector."

Bernie went off for a chair. Tess got up and dismantled the smoke detector. There it was.

"Oh my God, Tess. What has he been doing?"

"My guess is that he has been secretly taking photos of you. He has snapped you in the shower, coming out of the shower and undressing for bed. He probably intends to blackmail you at a future date."

"That's terrible. I feel deceived, defiled. How am I going to deal with this?"

She burst into tears.

"Calm down. Stay strong. The last thing you want to do at this time is confront him. I know it will be very difficult. Just try to carry on as normal for the time being while we make a plan."

"I'm at my wits' end. I didn't see this coming. I should have listened to you."

"Look, Bernie. I think you can turn the tables on Mr Dessie. He needs to be taught a lesson."

The two sisters made sure to put the cameras back exactly as they had found them. After some thought, Tess came up with the idea. They had a camera of their own installed in Bernie's bedroom. Over the next couple of weekends, they captured images of Dessie rifling through Bernie's clothes and dressing up in her underwear. Tess had Bernie document every call, every text and every conversation with Dessie.

After gathering a considerable amount of evidence, Bernie decided it was time to challenge her tormentor and deal with him once and for all. When he arrived on Friday evening, she was waiting for him in the hallway.

Dessie immediately sensed that all was not well.

"Is there something wrong, dear?"

"Indeed there is, Dessie. The game's up."

Dessie reddened.

"What are you talking about?"

"I'm talking about what you have been up to every weekend."

"I don't understand!"

"You have been messing with my wardrobe, dressing up in my underwear and videoing me in the shower. It's finished, Des."

"You can't do that, Bernie!" he sneered.

"Oh yes I can."

"I have lots of pictures of you in various states of undress. You wouldn't want anyone to see them, would you?" he announced triumphantly.

"No, I certainly wouldn't. And another thing. I'm sick of your controlling behaviour ever since I first met you."

Dessie laughed in her face.

"Haha. But you can't prove it! You'll be sorry, Bernie. You won't be able to show your face around here again."

Bernie beckoned him into the kitchen. Dessie was taken aback to see Tess sitting there. Bernie strode purposefully over to the kitchen table and pointed to her laptop and an open folder labelled "Evidence." He went deathly pale as he was presented with screenshots of his messages, photos of him going through her wardrobe and videos of her showering. She also showed him a draft email addressed to the Law Society, detailing his misconduct.

"You wouldn't dare," he stammered.

"I already have," Bernie replied.

"I've sent copies to the Law Society, the Gardaí, and a few journalists," she said calmly.

"Your career is over. And if you ever come near me again, I'll have you arrested. Now get out. I'm sick at the sight of you, you slimeball!"

As soon as he was gone, Tess rushed to her sister.

"You handled it brilliantly, Bernie. I'm so proud of you."

Bernie, who had been the picture of calm throughout, was now shaking like a leaf.

"I couldn't have done it without you, Tess."

"You certainly took the wind out of his sails."

Bernie still had to endure two days in court where she was the main witness. Dessie was found guilty, struck off by the Law Society, put on the sex offenders register and ordered to stay at least two kilometres from her property at all times. Bernie decided to focus on rebuilding her confidence and catching up on things she had recently neglected. Dating wasn't off the agenda, just postponed for a while.

The Pyramid Scheme

Jamie Osborne had been in China for over a year and had joined a local dating site. He had had several encounters to date, but nothing of consequence had come of it. The language barrier had been an ongoing problem. This time, luckily, the lady spoke English. She was a Chinese Canadian. Surely he was due a change of luck after a string of dating disasters.

He had just finished his last class for the day. The plan was to meet the lady at 6:30 pm in Yeuxia Park metro station. It was already after 6:00 and he had to get home, get dressed, and find his way there. He had been there before and was familiar with the layout of the place.

As he was having a shower, the phone rang. He rushed out of the bathroom with suds flying over his shoulder. It was indeed the said lady.

"Hi, this is Kirsty. I'm ready to go."

"Hello Kirsty. I'm sorry, I'm running a bit late."

"No worries. I'm with friends at the moment anyway."

"Right. Let's meet at Exit D and we can go for coffee. There's a Starbucks there. Look out for the China Hotel. The coffee shop is in the same building."

He took a taxi to save time. The metro would be busy at rush hour. While he was in the taxi, he got a text telling him she had arrived, and he assumed she was in Starbucks. On arrival, he went into the coffee shop and looked around. However, there was no visible sign of anyone who looked like her. He scanned the hallway, then wandered up to the hotel reception. Standing there, feeling utterly lost, a lady approached him.

"Good evening, sir. How are you?"

"I'm fine," he replied in an offhand kind of way. His mind was elsewhere.

"Where are you from, sir?" she enquired.

"I'm from Ireland," he snapped irritably.

She didn't flinch. "I have never been to Ireland but I studied in Scotland. I attended Strathclyde University for two years."

He moved away, but she kept walking after him.

She thought she recognised him but she couldn't quite place him. "Would you like to go for coffee?" she pleaded.

"No, thanks, I'm a little busy just now," he replied, gritting his teeth. Finally, he looked at her. She didn't really look like a hooker. Did she know him? Had he met her before? He kept moving and she kept following. She clearly didn't want to take NO for an answer.

Osborne then tried to reconnect with his date.

"Hi Kirsty. I'm here. Where are you?"

"Hi Jamie. I'm waiting for you at Exit B."

His jaw tightened. "I thought we had agreed to meet at Exit D. Can you come here?"

He knew he had been quite clear about their meeting point. Before he could say any more, she replied.

"My bag is so heavy. Can you come and help?"

"Okay Kirsty. Wait. I'll be a few minutes."

All the while, he was still being followed by the other lady. He pretended not to see her.

She saw this, but as she dropped back, she declared, "We'll meet again!"

He descended into the packed metro. Struggling through the crowds, it took some time to reach Exit B, which was on the far side of the road. He was again approached by the second lady while he was walking through the crowded subway. Again, he ignored her pleadings.

When he came out of Exit B, he couldn't see Kirsty. Then she called.

"Walk straight ahead towards the Guangdong TV Tower and you will soon see me. I'm with a group of people."

"Okay."

"I'm wearing a red suit."

He followed her directions, and it wasn't long until he spotted her – tall, sleek hair among several people who she obviously knew. They were all wearing suits, lanyards, and badges. Most of them were Chinese, but there were a few westerners there too. He had the feeling they had all been at some corporate event or meeting.

As Osborne approached, the group scattered with cheerful goodbyes all round. Kirsty turned and flashed him a dazzling smile. After briefly looking him over, she pointed in the direction of the metro.

"Ok, let's go," she thrust a heavy bag at him. "You're a lifesaver."

They went back into the metro, navigated through the throng, and came up at Exit D. With the extra weight, it suddenly struck Osborne what a long walk it was. Once inside the coffee shop, he ordered and paid for tea for both of them.

Unbeknownst to Osborne, Angela, the woman who'd accosted him earlier, had followed him and Kirsty into the coffee shop. Now, wearing sunglasses, she quietly slipped in behind them, taking a seat within earshot. From behind her dark lenses, she watched and listened.

No sooner had Osborne sat down than Kirsty began.

"How old do you think I am?" she asked.

"About thirty, I'd say."

"Actually, I'm thirty-eight," she corrected him triumphantly. "I guess you are about sixty-five."

He almost choked on his tea. "Fifty-seven, actually."

"I could make you look like a man of thirty."

"How would you do that?"

"If you follow my plan, you will be reinvigorated."

"How much will this cost?" he scoffed.

She didn't answer but pressed on. "Your libido will be like a man of twenty and, as a bonus, you will lose lots of weight."

This spiel lasted a good while, and she quoted a doctor from Arizona as the great expert who had devised this whole plan. She then named a list of athletes who had embraced it, not to mention countless beauty queens.

Osborne hadn't prepared for this. It was clearly a sales pitch.

She challenged him. "Look at my skin and hair!"

He looked at her hair, and to him, it resembled a horse's tail, it was so long and thick.

She went on. "As a teacher, you could introduce lots of people to me."

Red flags were waving. Alarm bells were ringing. This had to be a Pyramid/MLM scam.

He had read about it and indeed had seen it all before at first hand. Perhaps the scam wasn't known about in China and the American MLM people hoped to exploit that. Then he wondered if she really knew what she was involved in. Perhaps she didn't fully understand. If she was at entrance level, probably not.

He recalled having that same feeling many years before when a friend and he were invited to a marketing meeting by a prominent sporting figure. A large group of young men, all impeccably dressed in suits. The whole MLM scheme was introduced. It was water filters that time, and he had seen the scam straight away then, as he did now.

After some time, Osborne decided he may as well be direct with the lady.

"Am I at a business meeting or on a date?"

She laughed, unfazed. "Why not both? Imagine the new you in a month."

She went on. "People have to be on the same fitness level to be able to date. Since you haven't got to my level yet, you wouldn't be a suitable partner for me."

He laughed. "Wow, so that's me ruled out of your life!"

"Don't worry. If you follow the plan, the situation could be reviewed in a month's time."

"Yeah sure, a new man." He laughed right up into her face. "Let's be real, Kirsty. You're not interested in me. You just want a customer. I think I'll pass this time."

"Your loss," she called after him as he walked off.

He wandered around the China Hotel, trying to make sense of it. Talking to himself…

"How do I manage to find these kind of ladies one after the other?"

Angela felt a flicker of satisfaction. She knew something was off. She had watched Osborne stiffen, challenge Kirsty, then leave. Good on him. As he left, he turned, looked at Kirsty and shook his head. In that moment Angela recognised him – jamos67 from the dating site. They'd recently matched, but so far there had been no communication. Real life and online life had somehow collided.

She finished her iced tea, then casually followed him into the hotel bar. He was seated at the counter, staring into his lager, looking for answers that he knew weren't really there. She hesitated for a moment, then took the seat beside him.

This time he couldn't run. Up close, she was softer than he'd first thought: sharp-eyed but not unkind, her earlier persistence now replaced with something like amusement.

"I told you we'd meet again," she said with a smile.

Jamie took a breath, unsure whether to brace himself or relax.

"I didn't take that seriously."

"The date didn't work out then?" she teased, in a low, knowing voice.

He hesitated a moment. "You could say that. How did you know?"

"I was in Starbucks. Sitting just behind you. You were so preoccupied you never noticed. I had my shades on."

Osborne exhaled sharply. "You're not even trying to hide it." He studied the woman. "You followed us?"

She smiled a wry kind of smile. "Let's just say I was… curious. Then I realised I'd seen you before. We matched last week, but neither of us messaged."

"Really?" replied Osborne, on the defensive, while he racked his brain.

She appealed to him, "You don't remember me, do you? Doesn't your profile picture have the Guangzhou Tower in the background? Your handle is jamos67?"

Jamie blinked. He squinted at her, his cheeks flushing. "Ohhhh dear! I… I do apologise. Angela, isn't it? I'm Jamie. It's been a very long day."

"It certainly looks like it," Angela chuckled. "When I saw you earlier, you looked lost. And then, well, I followed you and your... companion... into the coffee shop." She took a sip of her own drink, a colourful cocktail.

"While your 'date' was giving her spiel, I did a little searching on my phone." Angela gestured towards her handbag. "Her company. It's exactly what you thought, Jamie. A classic MLM operation, preying on the unwary."

"So, you've seen this before too?" Jamie asked, a flicker of genuine connection in his gaze.

"Oh, plenty. Not personally caught up in one, thankfully, but I've certainly seen the damage they cause. Financially, emotionally... it's brutal." She paused, her expression softening. "And when I recognised you, the handsome guy from the dating site, looking so utterly bewildered by it all... I thought you might appreciate a friendly face, some confirmation."

Jamie picked up his glass, a smile finally crossing his face. "You have no idea. I thought I was losing my mind, a magnet for oddballs."

Angela had to laugh. "Well, you're not alone. And you're not crazy. Just unlucky with your choice of ladies, it appears."

Jamie clinked his glass against hers. He looked at her for a long time – he was taken by her shining eyes, her infectious laugh, her kindness. A disastrous evening now didn't feel so bad.

"Where do I go from here?" he asked abruptly.

She leaned over. "You mean where do we go from here!"

A World Unto Herself

Tom Brown first met Sofia from Philadelphia on a sunny Sunday afternoon in Milan. Father's Day. The date stuck out because neither of them mentioned it. Perhaps a reminder of a path not followed. Before meeting, they had chatted at length online, although in truth Brown didn't retain much of what had been said. They had arranged to meet for lunch on Piazza V Giornata.

She spotted him first.

"Tom?"

He turned, and there she was. She was wearing big sunglasses and a green dress, looking like she'd just stepped off a yacht.

"That's me."

"Great," she said, walking on ahead. "I booked this rooftop restaurant. Come on. The view is magnificent and the food isn't bad either."

Sofia was a small woman with blonde hair and blue eyes. She seemed to have broken her nose at some time in the past, but it wasn't a totally unattractive feature. She was supposedly about fifty-seven, but Brown suspected she was over sixty. Still younger than himself. He could tell she had been a very pretty girl in earlier years.

The restaurant was spacious, airy, and indeed had a spectacular view across the city. Over a four-course lunch and a bottle of red wine, Sofia unfurled her life story.

"My aunt left me this villa in Tuscany. Gorgeous, but now there's a dispute over ownership. I run an English training company here. And back in Philly, I was married for a short time. Big mistake."

Tom nodded. "What happened?"

She waved it off. "Long story. Let's just say we weren't compatible."

He raised his glass. "To a most beautiful lady."

She laughed. "And to men who show up on time. You passed the first test."

Tom blinked. "There was a test?"

"There's always a test."

She talked a lot about her business, her time in Italy, her experiences in Italy, her views on Italy, and her non-personal life experiences.

"Do you expect to win your court case?" Brown asked.

"I hope so. It better end soon. The lawyers are bleeding me dry."

"How's your business going?"

"No shortage of students. Teachers are the problem."

"How come?"

"Hard to find. Hard to deal with. Hard to keep."

Brown's concentration wasn't the best. He was distracted, taking in the view while enjoying the food, the wine, and the ambience of the restaurant. He also felt there was a little bit of information overload. He did like her spark, until she cut off the waiter mid-sentence to correct his Italian, then complained about the sun, her shoes, the chair she was sat on.

Eventually Sofia got up. "Let's go. I'll walk you to the metro."

She offered to share the bill, but Brown waved her away.

"It's okay. I'll get it."

At the metro station, Sofia surprised him. "You should come visit me at the villa this summer."

Brown nodded. "I'd love that."

They parted ways. He into the metro en route to Cremona, she presumably to her home.

Months passed with just the odd message. Sofia was caught up in legal wrangles and weekend work. They finally arranged a meeting in late November.

"I have to do some errands. Do you mind accompanying me?"

"That's fine."

"Would you like to go ice skating?"

"Well, it's something I haven't done in forty years. I don't know if it's a good idea."

"Maybe we could go to the spa. You would need to bring a swimsuit, clean trainers, and a gym outfit."

"Actually, I go to the gym myself every day. But I fancy a day off."

The idea of hauling a bag of gym gear to Milan and back didn't appeal to him.

"Okay. I got it. I'll go to the spa myself before meeting you. Then we can drive to Lake Como."

"Great idea," gushed Brown, signalling his enthusiasm. He had never been there and it was a place he desperately wanted to see.

"I'll pick you up at Coin about 2:30 p.m. The same place as last time."

On the occasion of their first encounter, it had been a balmy late spring afternoon. Now it was a dank, drizzly November day with grey skies. Even though he had got slightly lost, he was still early and ducked into a coffee shop for a quick caffè lungo.

It was 2:20 when he arrived at the meeting point. He went into Coin and wandered around. It was warmer in there. He spent some time looking around the men's department, although he was probably observing the customers and their goings-on more than the products on display.

Around 2:30 he went downstairs and positioned himself just inside the main door to await Sofia's arrival. He was standing right by the men's grooming department. The man working there tried to interest him in some hair product. Brown said nothing, pulled off his hat, and showed him his hairless head.

Time moved on, and Brown was looking around for signs of Sofia as it approached 2:40. He looked at his phone and, sure enough, he had a message and a missed call. She had driven past but couldn't see him and had gone off to park.

A few minutes later, Sofia breezed in.

"Sorry. I have to attend to some business in the make-up department."

Tom followed as she discussed eyeliner with a shop assistant. Someone had bought her a present of eyeliner, but she didn't like the colour. Brown stood idly by.

She then announced, "They don't do the colour I want. Now I have to go downstairs to get a refund."

Sofia was still muttering about the eyeliner. On the way down, the guy from the eyeliner department overtook them and demonstrated another product to her while they were on the escalator. Sofia had a heated discussion with him before waving him away.

She had to go in a queue. While they waited, she turned to Brown.

"We can't go to Como today. It's too late. We'll have a shopping day."

"Whatever you say!"

She then engaged in another long conversation with the shop assistant. As she completed her business, she had another idea.

"Let's start with a coffee."

Brown nodded. The coffee counter was just beside where they stood, and it was complimentary.

They both had decaf. Both agreed it tasted terrible.

There was one more counter to visit before leaving. More consultations, more purchases. Brown lugged her shopping bags to the car. It was packed with shopping, many bags visible on the back seat.

"Are you not worried about thieves?" he asked.

"Not in this area," she said dismissively.

Once inside the car, a lot of items had to be moved so Brown could get seated. He still had a box of cat food under his feet.

"You have a cat, I see."

"Yes. It's a rare breed. Very big ears."

"My mother keeps cats."

"This guy has one big weakness. He won't chase mice. A mouse once got into my villa and the cat sat looking at it. It made no move to pursue it."

Off they went in the car. Next stop was her office. A class was in progress, so they didn't linger.

Sofia grabbed three more bags and handed them to Brown.

She was getting ready for Christmas, and this was one of her few free days in the meantime.

Some things would have to be brought to the villa, where she intended to spend the Feast of the Nativity. These items went into the boot, and the rest into the back seat.

"Just throw them in anywhere," she commanded.

Then the retail odyssey resumed. They walked about 300 metres along the street and then into a store selling homeware. She immediately started inspecting bed sets. A bluish-coloured set was chosen to match the blue walls of the designated room. Then it was on to the towels, and this took a lot longer. The room these were intended for had yellow walls, so again it was a matching exercise.

There were two towels required, a big one and a smaller one. She found a nice big one, but there was no equivalent smaller one. She looked at several large towels, but it was the same each time. They didn't match the patterns on the smaller towels.

There were at least two consultants called at various stages and every towel in the place examined. In the end, she chose two towels that were pretty similar, but not identical. There was still a duvet required, although that negotiation proved to be much more straightforward and a sale quickly agreed.

All these goods were paid for and bagged. Brown was again given responsibility for the carriage back to the car, and again some stuff had to go in the boot and some in the back seat. The boot was full now.

"Coffee," she suggested.

"My foot is killing me," pleaded Tom.

She had an adrenaline rush going now and didn't hear him. She led them towards a distant coffee shop, only to find it closed. Plan B was now called for.

"There's a real Irish bar not far away," she offered.

"I'm not a great fan of real Irish bars. I prefer the unreal variety."

This remark appeared to go over her head. But it wasn't the first utterance that hadn't registered.

"There's another coffee shop about ten minutes' walk away," she assured him.

They set off. Within a few metres, Brown realised he couldn't go much further. His foot was giving him severe pain.

"Sorry, Sofia. I can't go much further. Let's just go to the Irish bar on Porta Romana."

This time she heard. So they turned on their heel.

Sofia was rattling on about all matters relating to her and her job.

"One guy is a rugby player. He doesn't want to work evenings or weekends. Interferes with his training."

"Oh dear. Isn't that when all the classes are on?"

"Exactly. Can't understand why he is given so few hours."

Brown's foot was now dominating his thoughts, and his good humour was wearing off. However, they arrived safely at the bar and entered. It was similar to a lot of these establishments, with a row of high stools along the bar, some occupied. There were a few small groups of people at tables dotted around the place, and the walls were covered in images of what Ireland might look like to the patron of a real Irish bar. James Joyce, the Aran Islands, and Guinness were all represented. And, of course, the obligatory English soccer match showing on multiple screens.

Sofia went to find a table while Brown went to the bar. The barmaid seemed to be Irish. He ordered tea for Sofia and a glass of Guinness for himself. The girl brought a pint of Guinness. He said nothing. He felt he had complained enough today, even if it was with good reason.

The Guinness was good, and Sofia launched into another long diatribe. Again, it was her employees, the Italian tax system, and her friend in the US who had it much better.

Brown couldn't get a word in. At one point he tried interjecting.

"Europe's social welfare—"

She cut him off, ranting about inefficiency.

His foot was throbbing and his patience waning. He didn't know what her plan was for later, but he had lost interest. She seemed to sense something was up.

"I'll walk you to the metro when you are leaving."

"I'd need to be on my way soon."

They were out of there a few minutes later. She showed him to the nearby metro station. They hugged on the corner before going their separate ways.

As the train pulled away from Porta Romana, Brown sat there staring at his own tired reflection. For the first time that day, he allowed himself to laugh. Quietly, almost soundlessly, but enough to turn a few heads. He opened his book, but found himself reading the same sentence over and over.

He thought about Sofia. Her stories, her relentless energy, shopping without end. It wasn't that she was unpleasant. Just... a world unto herself. One you could visit, but not live in. His phone remained silent. No message. No missed call. No thanks. No nothing. He wasn't surprised. Would it have been any different if they had gone to Como? He doubted it.

He exited at Centrale and limped his way to the regional platform. As he waited for the train to Cremona, his thoughts drifted to the big-eared cat that had no interest in mouse hunting. Somehow, that seemed to explain everything.

About the Author

Originally from a farming community in County Tyrone, Northern Ireland, John Devlin attended the Rainey Endowed School, where he played rugby for both his school and for Ulster. He studied briefly at Leeds University in the 1970s, then worked a range of jobs—from student barman and construction project manager to sports writer and editor. After completing a degree through the Open University, he went on to teach English abroad.

For many years John lived in County Galway, but a midlife crisis took him out of his comfort zone and led him overseas to teach English in France, Italy, China and Vietnam. He taught in training centres, schools and universities and enjoyed meeting the many colourful characters, both locals and expats, that he encountered at work and in the neighbourhood haunts.

A keen observer of people and situations, John has kept diaries throughout his life. He once joked that his notebook would one day become a book, little realising that throwaway comment would become reality. He remains a devoted sports fan, following both rugby and Gaelic football while overseas, often rising in the wee small hours to watch matches streamed live in Xi'an or Ho Chi Minh City.

A lifelong fan of traditional Irish music, he still catches the odd live gig wherever he can and was amused to hear his favourite jigs on the playlist in a shopping mall in Guangzhou. He has two daughters and a son, all living in Dublin and Galway. Now back in County Galway himself, he may yet get itchy feet and book that next flight to who knows where…

www.ingramcontent.com/pod-product-compliance
Ingram Content Group UK Ltd.
Pitfield, Milton Keynes, MK11 3LW, UK
UKHW022210210925
463152UK00006B/32

9 781918 039047